Form Criticism of the Old Testament

By
Gene M. Tucker

Fortress Press
Philadelphia

Library of Congress Catalog Number 72-154487

ISBN 0-8006-0177-7

Printed in the U.S.A.   AF 1-177

00 99   13 14 15 16 17 18 19 20 21

Editor's Foreword

The production of the Hebrew Bible was a long and complicated process. In all its stages, from beginning to end, it lasted well over a thousand years; and each attempt to describe it discloses more of its complexity.

Despite many changes in special aims and tasks, modern scholarship has persisted with great constancy in its intention of telling the story of how the Bible came to be. Its orientation has been historical and its efforts to describe the contents of the Old Testament and their history have developed three clearly distinguishable methods of study: literary criticism, form criticism, and tradition criticism. Each one of these is really a discipline in its own right. All are interested in the whole story; but each one constitutes a sort of crosscut attempt at giving its account of the whole. And so each one has developed its own techniques and methods of analysis, appropriate to the phenomena on which it concentrates.

Since they "dug in" at very different points in the complex legacy, and since they developed methods of scientific work as distinctive as their special tasks, these three disciplines sometimes give the impression of being arrayed against each other in mutually exclusive fashion. That is not the case; they are interrelated. All three want to contribute to the telling of one story. Their interrelationship is organic and logical. Each discipline lives off the questions that have baffled the other two. Since none of the three is able to ask or deal with all of the questions that must be asked and dealt with to tell the story of the making of the Old Testament, and since all want to tell that story, their relationships are complementary. It is thus fitting that these three small volumes, corresponding to the three disciplines of modern criticism, should appear under a single title, "Guides to Biblical Scholarship."

Literary criticism was the first on the scene. At the outset it was a special variation of textual study. Concentrating on the Book of Genesis, Astruc discovered a literary pattern related to the variant use of the divine names which led him to conclude that, in dealing with the era of the patriarchs, Moses had made use of more than one document or "source" in producing the first book of the Bible. There was an Elohist source and a Yahwist one. The variant use of the divine names came to an end in the third chapter of Exodus. However, using the characteristics of the sources discovered by means of it as criteria, scholars soon extended documentary source study into the entire Pentateuch, and to the Book of Isaiah!

With the movement that carries the name of Wellhausen, literary criticism took a new turn; having focused on the discovery of documentary sources and the marks of their identification, it now began to ask about the setting and motivation that had originally prompted the production of these separate units. One of the incidental by-products of this development was that literary criticism now often carried the popular name of "historical criticism," or "higher criticism," to differentiate it from textual criticism which was "lower!" Of more profound significance for our understanding of the meaning of the whole story was the fact that this movement assumed that the production of Scripture was conditioned historically not only by the fact that it had combined documents with a prior history of their own, but also that wider movements in human life had influenced their contents. Implicit questions about revelation and the inspiration of Scripture were made more pressing.

Historical criticism complicated the questions about documentary sources raised by the earlier phase of literary criticism; but it could not deal with them. For example, though there was general agreement that the Pentateuch combined four sources, there was no unanimity about precisely what belonged to each of these. More serious still were the disagreements about the antecedent history of each of the four. Did each combine two or more separate units? And could one detect the hand of the redactor who had combined them? Or was each of the four strands a single unit that had gone through several stages of annotation and editing? And how large a role had been played by the final redactor(s) who had given the Pentateuch or the Book of Isaiah their present forms? The riddles were growing in number and the frustration they produced called for a new beginning. It was in this context that form criticism arose.

In his famous essay, "The Problem of the Hexateuch," written in the thirties, G. von Rad tells how the old methods of literary criticism failed to deal with his questions. In his frustration the rubrics for the presentation of the offering of first fruits caught his attention. This text (Deuteronomy 26:1–11) was one of the relatively few in which the prescriptions for what is to be done in a situation are combined with the words to be recited. It was the form of the recital—an enumeration of the acts of God in Israel's history—that von Rad found most important; he called it a *Credo,* and he proceeded to build his interpretation of all of Israel's traditions around this form. Gunkel and Mowinckel were pioneers in form criticism who preceded von Rad; but what is striking about the case of von Rad is how the limitations of literary criticism landed him in form criticism.

Form criticism concentrates on primary categories of form rather than on documents: the hymn, the blessing, the legend, the lament, and many, many more. That is its most original contribution. It combines this concentration with the historical interest in setting and function first stressed by the historical critics of Wellhausen's day. Who used a given form? in what context? and for what purposes? Form criticism depends greatly on the results of research in such areas as cult and liturgy, social psychology, and anthropology, for the meaning of a given unit depends as much on its function in the life of the community as on the positive contents of its form. Indeed, many form critics would insist that this *Sitz im Leben* is of far greater importance than contents for our understanding; and all would probably agree that it is indispensable.

The internal tensions and bifurcations in the practice of form criticism parallel those we have noted in literary criticism. There a study of the documents themselves competed with an interest in describing the social and political scene in which they were written. Here the analysis of the forms and the exposition of their contents is crowded by a desire to describe the character and significance of the ceremonial that originally developed them. This distinction is classically illustrated by two pioneers in the form critical movement, Hermann Gunkel and his pupil, Sigmund Mowinckel. Both concentrated most of their work on the Book of Psalms. Gunkel assumed psalms were essentially personal and private compositions, even when produced to express a public or communal mood. Though he recognized that their forms were shaped in ancient cultic settings, he was less preoccupied with those settings and their role than with the thought of the authors of psalms. Mowinckel reversed the focus. He became a historian of religion and cult, assuming that psalms had been written for the sake of their role in the actual ceremonial of worship rather than simply for the sake of expressing the experience of an individual author. Mowinckel himself expressed the distinction in the original Norwegian title of his great work, *The Psalms in Israel's Worship*. He called it *Offersang og Sangoffer*, which can be translated "Song of sacrifice and Sacrifice of song." Gunkel had stressed the latter; the song was the thing. Mowinckel emphasized the former; the liturgy which the song was to serve.

Literary criticism dealt with units of the Bible, and with the historical settings in which the writing occurred. Form criticism deals with an earlier preliterary phase of the story. At that stage Israel made its public witness to its understanding of itself in its relation to God in a wide variety of fixed forms suited to oral communication: blessings, oaths, hymns, legends, commandments, and many, many more. Eventually the forms became embedded in Israel's literature. The process of self-definition took place in an almost endless variety of circumstances in relation to the family, the temple, the school, the courts, the realm of the state and diplomacy, commerce and trade—to name some of the primary orbits.

Sometimes a specific act of this endless process of self-definition involved only a single Israelite. In other instances many persons or recognized groups participated in this process. Very often, too, the whole community of Israel expressed itself in these specific occasions that gave shape to and confirmed the use of particular forms. Form criticism presupposes that, however unwittingly, all Israelites over many centuries contributed to the making of the Bible; that it was simply a result of their having had a communal existence as Israelites. The interest and intention of form criticism is analytical; it concentrates on detailed aspects of the common life and on the specific forms nurtured by them. There is an interest in the pristine structure of such forms which views all subsequent elaboration or mixing of forms in larger units as a sort of secondary development. There is less interest in telling the story of the making of the Bible as a whole than in describing separately a great number of "scenes" that are finally to be absorbed by that story. Form criticism does not really answer the questions of literary criticism about the editing and combining of documentary units. It puts them in parentheses while going behind them to an earlier stage in the process. There it discloses scenes in the history of the making of the Bible hitherto unknown, scenes in which the practices of common life rather than writing are conspicuous. Thus, for the time being, the unanswered questions left by literary criticism are relativized in their importance, and left untouched. But eventually they reassert themselves, for analysis of primary scenes alone is not capable of telling the story.

Tradition criticism—in New Testament studies the preferred term is "redaction criticism"—responds to a new urge to tell the whole story. Its intentions are synthetic and presuppose the analytic work of both literary and form criticism. Since it follows in the wake of both, it assumes that both oral and written continuities play a role in the shaping of the traditions that finally culminated in Scripture. Individual historians of tradition will vary with respect to the emphasis they place upon one or the other. A comparison of the work of Martin Noth with that of Ivan Engnell illustrates this variation rather well. More significant, perhaps, than their differences in approach and method—or in results—is the fact that both presuppose and use the results of the efforts of literary and form criticism. The proportional significance assigned to oral and written means of transmission, respectively, is a minor matter compared to the common recognition that the whole community, in all expressions of its existence, participated in giving shape to the tradition and in handing it on, generation after generation.

Form criticism concentrates on primary forms—on the beginnings of the shaping of the traditions that finally result in the Old Testament. Redaction criticism, as distinct from tradition history, deals with the very last stages of the editing that presents Scripture in its fixed or final form. Tradition criticism is interested in all the stages that lie in between form and redaction criticism, the history of a tradition which, in the Old Testament, spans more than a millennium. In New Testament studies, which deal in a time span less than a tenth as long, there is an understandable tendency to conflate the study of tradition with that of the final process of editing. The situation is very different with respect to the Old Testament where the history of tradition contains so many facets and stages, all of which can by no means be described as "redactional." Form criticism helps to make us aware of that.

Literary criticism tried to tell the story of the making of the Bible as a story of writing and editing. At the crest of its influence it had asked a great many questions about the history of this process which it found unanswerable on the basis of literary presuppositions alone. Form criticism introduced the presupposition that the making and transmission of the contents of the Bible had an oral as well as a written side to it. This has given tradition critics the sort of freedom and flexibility which literary criticism lacked, and from the lack of which it suffered. This freedom has resulted in promising new essays. As an example, one may refer to Martin Noth's proposal. He suggests that there was a Deuteronomic Historian, a single personality, who made use of all of the older materials contained in that part of the Old Testament that begins with Deuteronomy and ends with 2 Kings. This proposal was Noth's way of getting across some quite specific and personal notions about the meaning of Israel's history. Making this proposal depends on the sort of awareness of openness and freedom made possible by form criticism. Literary criticism had always contemplated the tying together of the material in these books as a process carried on by a series of "Deuteronomic editors," conforming to the notion that the growth of tradition was by a process of writing, only. Noth's imagination and skill as a historian of tradition who presupposes a more open situation because of the oral character of much in the tradition enable him to endow this large section of the Old Testament with a freshness, a pointed clarity, and a unity such as it never had before.

It becomes increasingly clear that the three disciplines featured in this series are interdependent, as well as distinct. They all want to tell the same story; and they need each other's help in doing so. And they can help each other because, as we said at the outset, the orientation of all three is historical.

The historicality of the Bible, that is, the conditioned character of its contents, a conditioned-ness which makes them dependent upon all kinds of human limitations and situations in precisely the same way as the legacies of all sorts of historical traditions, is an assumption of modern criticism throughout. That assumption makes it modern. At the outset the assumption was held very tentatively, even fearfully, and in relatively circumscribed fashion.

It asserted itself in the face of venerable traditions of dogma and confessional authority that equated the form of the contents of Scripture, its verbal conceptualizations, with the divine absolute. But the asssumptions so gingerly held at the outset were to vindicate their tenability and importance in the process. The Bible is a far more historical book than the pioneers of historical criticism ever dreamed; and we are aware of this precisely because what they began continued: from literary criticism, to form criticism, to tradition criticism. In one way or another, over a period of more than a thousand years, the whole cultural setting of the ancient world of the Near East and every Israelite in all those centuries had some sort of a hand in the making of the Bible.

Needless to say, the impact of these developments on theology has been tremendous and continues as a powerful influence today. The word of God in relation to Scripture, as well as in relation to the church and the world, is being redefined and conceptualized in dynamic, fresh ways today because of the theological implications of modern criticism. Criticism set out to tell the story of the Bible. It did not intend to deal with theology, let alone launch new movements in theology. Nevertheless, however unintentionally, it did both.

J. Coert Rylaarsdam

Contents

Preface

Form criticism is one of the methods by which the student of the Bible can shed light upon the Old Testament. Specifically, it offers ways of gaining insight into the oral tradition which lies behind most of the individual passages of the Old Testament. By examining each passage in terms of its structure and genre the student gains a fuller understanding of its meaning and intention, and of its setting in the life of ancient Israel. That is the purpose of form criticism: To relate the texts before us to the living people and institutions of ancient Israel.

One of my assumptions in writing this book is that form criticism is not an esoteric enterprise reserved for a few scholars in their studies, but, rather, that it has significant contributions to make to any serious reader of the Old Testament. I have also assumed that the reader will benefit more from learning how to ask the form critical questions than from simply reading the results or conclusions of form critical research, so I have attempted here to emphasize methodology itself.

It is not only of necessity but by intention that this work stands in a tradition and a community of scholarship. Consequently, the size of this little volume is no measure of the magnitude of my indebtedness and gratitude to other scholars and friends. I am deeply grateful to Brevard S. Childs, who first introduced me to form criticism and has continued to provide encouragement and guidance; to Bernhard W. Anderson, who made some very helpful suggestions at an early stage in the preparation of this book; to a former colleague, Harmon L. Smith, who read portions of the typescript from the perspective of the nonspecialist and offered incisive suggestions; and to J. Coert Rylaarsdam, the editor of this series, whose assistance at each stage in the writing is gratefully acknowledged.

Much of what has been written here has arisen out of the discussions and work of the Old Testament Form Critical Project, which is preparing *The Interpreter's Handbook of Old Testament Form Criticism* (Rolf Knierim and Gene M. Tucker, editors; to be published in two volumes by Abingdon Press in 1975). The methodology presented here follows in general the patterns being developed by that project. I owe a deep debt of gratitude to the co-editor, Rolf Knierim, with whom I have worked closely for five years, and to each member of the team: George W. Coats, Erhard Gerstenberger, Dennis J. McCarthy, S.J., Roland E. Murphy, O.Carm., Kent Richards, H. Eberhard von Waldow, and J. William Whedbee.

Finally this book is dedicated with affection and appreciation to my father-in-law, Jarrett E. Williams, M.D., a layman who is not only deeply interested in the Bible but in biblical criticism as well.

Abbreviations

BZAW	*Beihefte zur Zeitschrift für die Alttestamentliche Wissenschaft*
CBQ	*Catholic Biblical Quarterly*
JBL	*Journal of Biblical Literature*
RGG	*Die Religion in Geschichte und Gegenwart*
SBT	*Studies in Biblical Theology*
VT	*Vetus Testamentum*
WMANT	*Wissenschaftliche Monographien zum Alten und Neuen Testament*
ZTK	*Zeitschrift für Theologie und Kirche*

I.

The Form

Critical Method

The Old Testament stands before us today as literature, a virtual library of diverse literary types and compositions; but most of that literature arose as the spoken word and
was first transmitted in the oral tradition. Because the Old
Testament is literature, literary methods must be used in
order to understand it: and since most of the Old Testament
had a long oral or preliterary tradition, a full understanding of its literature requires an understanding of that oral
tradition.

To speak of the Old Testament as literature is not, of
course, to exhaust its meaning or the possibilities for its legit-
imate contemporary interpretation. We must recognize, however, that this book arose out of the rich life of a particular
people. Any attempt to understand the Old Testament which
does not begin with a knowledge of what its various parts
meant in and to the life of that people is therefore destined
to be incomplete and perhaps even false.

One of the methods of understanding the meaning and
history of the Old Testament in the life of ancient Israel is
form criticism. Form criticism is a method of analyzing and
interpreting the literature of the Old Testament through a
study of its literary types or genres. In particular, form
criticism is a means of identifying the genres of that literature,
their structures, intentions and settings in order to understand
the oral stage of their development.

Before turning to the Old Testament itself we may begin
to understand the nature of genres of speech and literature by

observing how they function in our own experience, for they are common to all cultures.

If one reads the words, "Once upon a time . . . ," at the beginning of a story he probably knows already what type of literature he is reading. He will expect the story to conclude with the expression, "And they lived happily ever after." He knows, furthermore, that these beginning and concluding expressions are typical formulas of the fairy tale, when and where such stories normally would be used, and by whom. The fairy tale is a literary genre widely used in both ancient and modern times by parents to entertain and to teach their children. Today we are most likely to read such stories to our children, but before the widespread use of books the stories would have been presented orally. The genre, *fairy tale*, undoubtedly arose in the oral tradition.

From the moment when we arise and greet one another with the expression, "Good morning," until we retire with the words, "Good night," we constantly hear and use stereotyped expressions or formulas. Common genres—or types—of speech and literature meet our eyes and ears each hour that we encounter human language. Furthermore, not only do we shape such genres to suit our particular purposes, but our language and our thought are shaped by them. Our friends may tell us *jokes*, or we may hear a *lecture*, or see the presentation of a *play*, or read in the newspaper a *news story*, an *editorial*, or a *letter to the editor*. For entertainment or edification we may read a *novel*, a *short story*, or a *poem*. Each of these genres has its own distinctive structure, its particular setting in life, and its special intention or function. Each genre also has a particular mood or tone appropriate to its setting and function, and a content which, though it may vary considerably in details, is nonetheless inextricably united with the particular genre.

Genres of speech and literature, as well as the formulas within them, arise and become stereotyped because of recurring situations in human life. For example, businessmen repeatedly write letters in the course of their work. The recurring situations have produced a stock of formulas and types of correspondence from which each individual businessman may and does draw when a particular need presents itself. It would not occur to a businessman, writing concerning supplies for his firm, to begin his letter, "My dearest one," and conclude with "Love. . . ." He will instead use the language, formulas and structure of the business letter. His decision to use one genre (the business letter) rather than the other (the love letter) is determined primarily by his situation and his intention or purpose for writing. It is unlikely that he will reflect on the decision, or even be aware of it, since the situation and intention quite normally determine which genre is appropriate and which is not. Each genre, then, arises in and is appropriate for use in a particular situation.

Genres, as situations, may be defined both broadly and very specifically. Within the broad category *business letter* there are many different genres, each appropriate for a certain setting and purpose. Within the broad category *novel* one may identify *historical novels, mystery stories, romances*, and many others. And within the broad category *television program* one may recognize such diverse genres as *situation comedies, dramas, Westerns, documentaries, musicals, news programs*, and others. Very frequently a genre may consist of a mixture of elements from two or more other types. For example, a business letter stating the terms and conditions of a person's employment includes elements of a contract and may be considered both a letter and a contract.

When we are able to see that our own language is shaped by the structures and formulas of our genres of speech and literature we can understand how such conventional genres exerted a powerful influence in ancient cultures, including that of ancient Israel. Folk literature, which ordinarily arises and is transmitted orally, is even more subject to traditional conventions than is modern literature. This is true primarily because ancient story tellers and speakers generally lacked a certain factor which is important to their modern counterparts, namely, a literary self-consciousness. A modern writer usually wants his productions to be marked by his individual style, and he wants it to be understood clearly that what he has written is his own work. In folk literature, however, there is little concern for authorship and individuality. The literature is the common property of the community, and therefore more subject to the traditional literary patterns of that community.

Thus, while individuals—and often very creative individuals—originated and contributed to particular stories, it is usually impossible to identify the "authors" of folk literature. To the "purist," the only true folk song is one which cannot be traced back to a particular composer.

Furthermore, in cultures where there are few books and comparatively few written records, the conventional structures and formulas are more persistent and pervasive—indeed, more necessary—than they are in a highly literate culture. Stories and sayings which must be passed down orally are cast into traditional molds. Even the activities of everyday life relied heavily upon formulas and established genres. For instance, a modern contract is validated by being committed to writing, signed and witnessed: but in the early history of Israel (and perhaps later also) the same function was accomplished orally through the use of set formulas. The contract was "notarized" not by signature and seals on a written document but by the oral expression of the agreement made in public and attested by the witnesses present " in the gate," where both civil and criminal legal proceedings transpired. The agreement was "notarized" when one party said to the witnesses, "You are witnesses," and they replied, "We are witnesses." (Cf. Ruth 4:1–12.)[1]

Thus in cultures less dominated by the written word than is ours, in particular, the culture which produced the Old Testament, many of the functions of our written documents and literature were accomplished by oral "documents" and oral "literature" which adhered closely to traditional formulas and genres.

If we wish, then, to understand the Old Testament, and in particular to understand the background and preliterary history of its literature, we must pose the questions raised by form criticism.

THE BEGINNING OF OLD TESTAMENT FORM CRITICISM

The attempt to understand the Old Testament through a study of its literary and oral genres is not new. The first man

---

1. Gene M. Tucker, "Witnesses and 'Dates' in Israelite Contracts," *CBQ* 28(1966): 42–45; and H. J. Boecker, *Redeformen des Rechtslebens im Alten Testament*, WMANT 14 (Neukirchen: Neukirchener, 1964): 160–75.

to study these types systematically was Hermann Gunkel (1862–1932). Gunkel was influenced by the studies of folk-lore initiated by Jakob and Wilhelm Grimm, who had collected the folk traditions of the German people and classified them as fairy tales, myths, sagas and legends.[2]

He was also impressed by the wealth of newly discovered and translated religious literature from Mesopotamia and Egypt which at points exhibited striking similarities to the Old Testament. Gunkel, who was interested in Old Testament literature and above all in its history, recognized at the beginning of his career that much of the Old Testament itself was folk literature; that is, it had originated orally. He also recognized that it contained literary types which had been influenced by those of other cultures.

When he began his work in the last years of the nineteenth century, biblical scholarship was dominated by source criticism. By the turn of the century source critics, who had set out to answer the questions of the authorship and date of the literary documents of the Bible, were attempting to write the complete history of the literature of the Old Testament. Gunkel's work was stimulated by this concern with the history of literature,[3] but he soon began to demonstrate that such a history could not be written without a new approach.[4]

While he recognized the necessity of determining the date and authorship of a given book or document when possible, he argued that a history of Old Testament literature limited to the biographies of the writers was inadequate. For the most part the writers collected and used material which itself had a long prehistory of oral transmission and development. Source critics had been interested in exploring and understanding the distinctive styles of individual writers, but Gunkel was impressed with the great similarities of expression: "In

---

2. It is often popularly assumed that the Grimm brothers *wrote* the fairy tales which bear their names, but this was not the case. They simply collected and committed to writing stories which had circulated orally for generations.
3. Cf. H. J. Kraus, *Geschichte der historisch-kritischen Erforschung des Alten Testaments,* 2nd ed. (Neukirchen: Neukirchener, 1969), pp. 341 ff.
4. Gunkel described this approach in two very important little works: "Die israelitische Literatur," in *Die Kultur der Gegenwart,* 1. 7, pp. 51–102; and "Fundamental Problems of Hebrew Literary History," in *What Remains of the Old Testament,* pp. 57–68.

the Psalms, for instance, we find an extraordinary sameness of content—in different Psalms we find the same thoughts, moods, forms of expression, metaphors, rhetorical figures, phrases."[5] These similarities of expression stem from the fact that the same genres of speech and literature had been used over and over again. Thus Gunkel perceived that one could write that more comprehensive history of Old Testament literature only by understanding the background and history of its literary types.

Gunkel then outlined in broad terms the main literary types in the Old Testament, describing them under the general rubrics of prose or poetry, setting each into its historical framework, and suggesting its place in the life of ancient Israel. At the outset he could give no more than a general outline of the genres, but he succeeded in placing before biblical scholarship its task for the coming decades, namely, the precise and detailed study of the types of biblical literature (which includes the New Testament as well as the Old). In later years, Gunkel himself made great strides in the new discipline, especially in his commentaries on Genesis and Psalms. But above all he set the pattern for much of the work that was to be done and is still being done.

BASIC PRINCIPLES AND AIMS OF FORM CRITICISM

The first basic principle of form criticism is that most of the literature of the Old Testament had a long and often complicated oral prehistory. Though all of the material eventually passed through the hands of writers, collectors, or editors, much of it arose as folk literature with no identifiable author. This observation applies to material as diverse as the narratives in the Pentateuch and the sayings in the Book of Proverbs. Even where the originator of the material can be identified (for example, in many cases in the prophetic books), often that man was first a speaker and secondarily—if at all— a writer.

The dependence on the spoken word is abundantly clear in the prophetic books, for the prophets were primarily men

---

5. Gunkel, "Fundamental Problems of Hebrew Literary History," pp. 58–59.

who *spoke* the word of God which had been revealed to them. Over and over we discover references to this word which they call upon the people to hear. But the situations surrounding the delivery of their speeches seldom are described unless some remarkable event occurs, such as strong opposition to their right to speak, as in Jeremiah 26:7 ff., 7:1 ff., and Amos 7:10–17. When there are references to written prophetic words it is clear that something new and noteworthy has occurred. When Jeremiah was "debarred from going to the house of the Lord" (Jer. 36:5), he dictated to Baruch the speeches which he had given up to that time and instructed the scribe to "go, and on a fast day in the hearing of all the people in the Lord's house you shall read the words of the Lord from the scroll which you have written at my dictation" (Jer. 36:6). When the king responded by burning the scroll, Jeremiah dictated the speeches again, and "many similar words were added to them" (Jer. 36:32, cf. also 30:2). This account gives us a good indication of one of the ways the transition from oral speeches to prophetic books took place. A similar situation and result may be reflected in Isaiah's instructions: "Bind up the testimony, seal the teaching among my disciples" (Isa. 8:16).

Prophetic speech is not the only genre, however. The oral roots of other genres of Old Testament literature can also be recognized. The Book of Psalms is a collection of songs which were sung in worship, where many of them continue to be used today. The individual sayings in the Book of Proverbs arose for the most part either as short, practical and memorable observations about life or as the instructions of "wise men." One even finds an occasional reference to the oral method of teaching (Prov. 22:17; 23:12; 15:2 ff.), as well as to the writing down of sayings (Prov. 22:20–21). The oral heritage of songs and sayings reveals itself not only in the allusions to the use of such types, but by their very nature: songs are made to be sung and sayings to be said.

The background of the narrative material in the spoken word is no less evident. All ancient—and even primitive—cultures had a body of oral "literature"—that is, folklore—long before they developed written records and literature. In the Old Testament narrative works there are occasional references to "books" which were used by the editors and writers of the present books, but often even the "books" which they used (such as the Book of Jashar, mentioned in Jos. 10:13) were collections of folk material. This is not to deny that many parts of the Old Testament, even some early parts, arose as written literature; indeed, such almost certainly was the case in the story of David's later life (the Throne Succession history: 2 Sam. 9–20, 1 Kings 1–2).

Though the techniques of form criticism are especially useful in the analysis of the oral stage of biblical literature, they are applicable as well to the written stages and to material which arose as literature. The form critical analysis helps, among other things, to determine whether a particular book or unit arose orally or in writing, and to understand the situation in which a specific piece arose.

A second basic principle of form criticism concerns the history of genres and the power of oral tradition: There is a certain tenacity in the genres, but also flexibility and change as they develop. Another way of putting the principle is to say that genres arise, develop, flourish and eventually decay, often giving rise in the process to mutations or new genres. Once one has come to recognize, for example, the prophetic speech announcing judgment on the nation, he can see the same genre in Amos, Jeremiah, Ezekiel, and even remnants of such speeches in the early narratives concerning the preclassical prophets in the Books of Samuel and Kings. However, while it is clear that the same genre was used throughout a long history, it is equally clear that there are variations from case to case. The speeches in Jeremiah are ordinarily longer than those in Amos, and those in Ezekiel have taken on a decidedly literary flavor. Two factors account for the variations: the historical development of the genre, and the individuality of each prophet. Carrying the point a step further, one can observe that prophetic speeches and prophetic literature as a living process eventually came to an end. Their place was taken by apocalyptic literature, which developed in part out of prophetic genres and in part out of foreign influences, in short, because of significant changes in Israel's (now Judaism's) situation. Certain genres and certain stages in the development of genres belong, then, to specific periods and situations.

A third principle of form criticism is that each genre originates in a particular setting or *Sitz im Leben* and that this setting can be recovered through a study of the genre itself. The examples given above (see pp. 2 ff.) demonstrate this point with modern genres and contemporary situations. Since we know much less about ancient Israel's history and institutions, in some cases we can reach only very general conclusions concerning the setting of certain genres (for example, that virtually all the Psalms were used in cultic situations). In other cases, however, we can be very specific (for example, showing that a particular type of hymn was used in a particular kind of worship service, or even in a certain part of that service).

Careful study often reveals that a particular story or speech has been alive in more than one setting. In the speeches of the prophets, for instance, one finds genres which originated in the worship or the court or elsewhere. So those speeches reflect at least three distinct settings: the background in cultic, legal or other institutions; the prophetic speech itself as an event in the life of the prophet and of Israel; and the situation in which the speech was collected and perhaps edited.

The goals of form criticism, then, are twofold. First, it attempts to recover the full, living history of Old Testament literature, especially to gain insight into its oral stage of development, and to place all the stages of development into their settings in the life of Israel. Second, form criticism is a tool of exegesis *per se*. It attempts to facilitate the full understanding and interpretation of what is essentially ancient religious literature that has a long and complicated history and prehistory. An awareness of the literary history of that material is an essential foundation for exegesis—for such an awareness may show that a given passage had not one meaning but various meanings through numerous stages of development— but it is no substitute for interpretation.[6] Form criticism attempts to aid in the exegesis and interpretation of biblical texts by asking very direct questions concerning the nature and meaning of those texts.

---

6. Gene M. Tucker, Review of Klaus Koch, *Was Ist Formgeschichte? Neue Wege der Bibelexegese* (Neukirchen: Neukirchener, 1964); in *Dialog* 5 (1966): 147. The book has now appeared in English as Koch, *The Growth of the Biblical Tradition*.

THE METHODS OF OLD TESTAMENT FORM CRITICISM

How does one learn about the preliterary history of the Old Testament literature and the situations in which it arose? The problem and the method may be illustrated by means of a fictitious example which is most directly applicable to the prophetic books, but the basic principles apply throughout the Old Testament.

Imagine, if you will, a pastor who, throughout his career, has presented sermons of all kinds for various occasions. Some were exegetical sermons on diverse biblical texts; others were topical sermons of various kinds. In addition he wrote and presented numerous speeches and lectures of different types: Sunday school lessons, prayers, addresses to the local Rotary Club, commencement addresses, and others. The man failed to date or label most of his manuscripts, but simply placed them one after another into his files. Upon the death of the now famous preacher, a friend decided that his works should not be lost, so he collected the manuscripts and copied them. Perhaps he attempted to arrange the material topically or chronologically. But he simply ran all the works together without divisions or headings, so that there was no indication of the date or circumstances or even the title of each work.

If we come along later and want to understand the great man's thought as well as his life and times we are faced with difficulties. We must begin by making sense of his writings, but how?

Our first task will be to disentangle the various speeches from one another, that is, to determine the appropriate units. Our first clues to the units will be the typical introductory and concluding formulas for different kinds of material. For example, we will expect the prayers to begin, "Our Father. . . ." And our task will be much easier if his sermons as well as his prayers conclude with "Amen." Or he may have begun and concluded each sermon with a set formula. By the time we have located all the introductory and concluding formulas we will have isolated many of the original units as they were presented. Another aid in determining the units will be the typical structures and styles of each different type of speech. His sermons will follow different outlines, but all of them will be different from his prayers and lectures. The prayers will be written in the second person, addressing God, the sermons will be addressed to the congregation, and some Sunday school lessons will be addressed to little children. Each type will reflect a different situation and will have been prepared for a different purpose.

After we have isolated the different units we will need to study each one carefully. It will be necessary to understand its structure and its type as well as its situation and intention or purpose. Then we will be in a position to understand the thought as well as the life and times of the preacher through his writings.

In modern times our example may be an unlikely story. It is very improbable that the works of a great man would be handled so carelessly and come to us in such disorder. But this was precisely the case in ancient Israel, especially in the words of the prophets. The major difference between our example and the Old Testament literature is that the latter is even more complex. Consider the prophets, for example. Some of their speeches were dictated to scribes, some were remembered and later written down by the prophet himself or his disciples, and some were first composed and then delivered orally or circulated perhaps as tracts or pamphlets (as in some of the latest books). Furthermore, as the words were collected and copied to form books, there was little concern to distinguish between the prophet's original words and those of later generations.

We know the conventions of our modern types of speech and literature, but we must look carefully to discern the conventional genres of ancient Israel. These genres are not defined and described anywhere in the Old Testament itself, but they were just as familiar to those who created the Old Testament as were the rules of Hebrew grammar (which they also failed to hand down to us!).[7]

The steps in the form critical analysis of a biblical text may be arranged systematically under four headings: (1) analysis of the structure, (2) description of the genre, (3) definition of the setting or settings, and (4) statement of the intention, purpose, or function of the text. Though it is necessary to

---

7. Gunkel, "Fundamental Problems of Hebrew Literary History," pp. 60–61.

consider each point in order, no step should be taken in isolation from the others; all are parts of the form critical attempt to analyze and describe the history and nature of a given segment of the Old Testament literature. It should be emphasized here that this methodology focuses upon the analysis of particular biblical passages—or even larger bodies of material —rather than the construction and description of hypothetical, ideal genres.[8]

At this point some observations concerning terminology are in order. In the methodology described here, the terms *structure* and *genre* represent an attempt to bring precision and clarity to a point which has been assumed in form critical methodology but seldom articulated clearly and often obscured by the term *form*. *Structure* refers to the outline, the pattern or the schema of a given piece of literature or a given genre; *genre*, on the other hand, refers to the type or *Gattung* itself. The two concepts are *distinct but inseparable* when one looks at literature as a form critic: some confusion has resulted from the tendency to use the term *form* to mean both structure and genre. If the term *form* is used in reference to genre or *Gattung*, it should be made clear that the word has taken on a secondary connotation.[9]

Each step may now be considered in turn as it is applied to representative biblical texts in Chapter II.

Structure. It has already been pointed out that the first step in a form critical analysis is the determination of the appropriate, original unit for analysis. It has often been assumed that form criticism deals only or primarily with very small units, and thus tends to be atomistic. But this is by no means the case. An entire prophetic book is an appropriate unit for form critical analysis, since that completed book represents a stage in the growth of the material. And, as Gerhard von Rad has shown, even the entire Hexateuch (Genesis through Joshua) is a unit which should be submitted to form

8. For general descriptions of the genres of Old Testament literature one may consult the recent introductions to the Old Testament. See especially G. Fohrer, *Introduction to the Old Testament*, initiated by E. Sellin, trans. David E. Green (Nashville: Abingdon, 1968), or O. Eissfeldt, *The Old Testament: An Introduction*, trans. Peter R. Ackroyd (New York: Harper & Row, 1965).
9. Gene M. Tucker, *Dialog* 5 (1966): 145.

critical analysis.[10] But we must also attempt to find in these larger units the original speeches or stories which were combined to make up that unit.

Some of the means for determining units have been mentioned above. One first attempts to discover the customary beginning and concluding formulas for each genre. Prophetic books begin with superscriptions: "The word of the Lord that came to Micah of Moresheth in the days of Jotham, Ahaz, Hezekiah, kings of Judah, which he saw concerning Samaria and Jerusalem" (Micah 1:1). Individual prophetic speeches begin with various formulas, such as the call to attention, "Hear this word, you cows of Bashan . . ." (Amos 4:1), or the word event formula, "The word of the Lord came to me . . ." (Ezek. 6:1). Each particular genre therefore is characterized by a certain introduction, and often by a certain conclusion.

Even when the introductory and concluding formulas are missing or unclear, one may still distinguish the units from one another by recognizing the conventional patterns of different genres. The poetic parallelism and symmetry of a series of lines often betray the limits of a particular song, speech or poem. Different types of stories or speeches follow different structures, and a change in genre may indicate that a new unit has begun. Moreover, we may distinguish units from one another by changes in content, style, mood and tone, or person and tense.

Once the divisions have been made, the form critic turns his attention to the structure of each specific unit. He outlines that structure, giving attention primarily to matters of form and secondarily to matters of content. He discovers how the passage before him follows the conventional structure of its genre, and how it differs. No two examples of a genre are exactly alike.

Genre. Our concern at this point in the analysis is to define and describe a particular text as an example of one or another genre. The description may move from very broad observations to more precise ones. We can begin by noting whether the material is prose or poetry, and then what kind of prose

---

10. Gerhard von Rad, "The Form Critical Problem of the Hexateuch," in *The Problem of the Hexateuch and Other Essays*, pp. 1–78.

or poetry. For instance, with a given psalm one may observe that it is lyric poetry, then that it is a hymn, and finally that it is a specific type of hymn of praise. The form critic's goal at this stage is to find the most appropriate and specific category into which the unit should be placed.

Since genres are not *sui generis* or unique, we will expect to find more than one example of each in the biblical literature. More importantly, we cannot fully understand a particular example of a genre without comparing it with other examples. This comparison will reveal which elements in the genre are more or less constant (and therefore comprise the formal elements), and which elements are variable. In such comparisons we are not limited to the biblical material itself, but we may also include extrabiblical material from ancient Near Eastern literature. Indeed, considerable light has been shed, for example, on the structure of the ancient Israelite covenant ceremony by comparing the accounts of such ceremonies with the ancient Near Eastern treaties.

There are, of course, *sui generis* or unique elements in each particular biblical passage, but these are created by the individuality of a particular writer, the content of the material, or the specific situation which lies behind the written words. The form critical classification of that passage does not obscure this uniqueness: instead, it helps to make individuality and uniqueness clear by distinguishing them from the stereotyped or conventional aspects of the genre.

Some types of speech or literature are more stereotyped or formalized than others. The structure of a conversation is much more flexible, for example, than that of a legal argument before a court: and the limerick follows rather rigid schemes of meter and rhyme while there are many other specific genres which use both meter and rhyme much more freely. Acrostic psalms are examples of poetry which follow rather definite outlines: each line must begin with a successive letter of the alphabet.

As one identifies and describes the genre of his text, he will also be alert to the short formulas within a particular genre: for example, to the messenger formula, "Thus says the Lord," in prophetic speeches, or to the curse formulas in Deuteronomy 27:15 ff. Formulas actually are short genres. Each stereotyped formula, as each genre, has a certain setting in which it originated and in which it customarily was used, but just as genres could be borrowed from one setting for use in another, so could formulas. To illustrate: When Amos says, "Come to Bethel, and transgress; to Gilgal, and multiply transgression," he has borrowed a cultic formula (the call to worship), changed it, and used it in a prophetic speech in criticism of the cult.

Setting. "Every ancient literary type," said Gunkel, "originally belonged to a quite definite side of the national life of Israel."[11] The term *setting* is used here for Gunkel's phrase *Sitz im Leben,* which has become a common expression in biblical studies. The term refers to the sociological situation which produced and maintained the various genres—such as the activity of the cult, the legal institutions, the "school," the family life, the tribal institutions, or the institutions and customs of the royal court. *Setting,* as used here, does not refer primarily to the date or historical period of the genres; though the historical situation is one aspect of the setting. For example, if we identify a genre with the life of the first temple, we will know that it belongs to the era between Solomon and the exile. We can, in fact, often establish the relative chronology of the genres themselves, even to the point of determining the influence of historical events on those genres. However, the task of dating specific biblical documents is basically that of source criticism.

The description of the setting should follow quite directly from a correct description of the genre itself: Hymns belong in worship and laws belong to the legal process. Nevertheless, since we know much less about ancient Israel's institutions than we do about our own, we must examine carefully each genre—and each example of that genre—for evidence of its setting. Not all of Israel's laws stem from what we would consider the law court. Many of them arose from and were used in acts of worship, and all of Israel's laws were placed eventually into the context of religious institutions.

Often the genres contain quite definite clues to their settings. There may be allusions within a passage to the activities which surrounded the use of certain genres. Joshua 24:1-28, for

---

11. Gunkel, "Fundamental Problems of Hebrew Literary History," p. 61.

example, describes a ceremony for the renewal of the covenant: and in doing so mentions not only what was said at that ceremony but some of the things which were done. By comparing this description with others, it has been possible to determine that the account reflects a cultic institution and a situation which must have been repeated many times in Israel, namely, the covenant renewal ceremony.

When we ask the basic questions of a genre, "Who is speaking and who are the listeners,"[12] we gain insight into the circumstances and hence into the setting of the genre. Furthermore, the structure of the genre itself often reveals details of the setting, as in the case of Psalm 136. The refrain of this psalm, which is constantly repeated in the second half of each verse, shows that the chapter is a litany in two parts: one for the priest or priestly choir and the other for the congregation. Other indications of the setting include the mood and tone (the dirge at the funeral differs sharply from the love song at a wedding), and the intention or purpose of the genre (sermons attempt to admonish, to teach or interpret; but hymns mean to express praise or thanksgiving).

Where a passage contains more than one genre, it will also reflect more than one setting—as is the case with originally cultic, legal or wisdom material which has been appropriated, adapted or copied for use in prophetic speeches.

Intention. Just as every genre arises in a particular situation, it also arises in order to fulfill some particular purpose, and it survives because it continues to be needed for that purpose. At this point in the investigation, then, we attempt to determine the intention of the genre. But raising this question is not an attempt to read the mind of the ancient writer or speaker; it is rather an attempt to discern what function the genre served or attempted to serve in its ancient setting. We must focus attention both upon the intention of the genre in general and upon the specific intention of the particular example before us. For example, the intention of etiological sagas is to explain existing phenomena by reference to an event in the past. But in particular examples of such sagas the etiological inten-

---

12. Cf. ibid., p. 62.

tion may be secondary to another, perhaps a historical, intention.

The term *intention* has been chosen here in preference to "function" because it is both easier and more relevant to determine the effect which was intended than that actually accomplished. A particular story may have been circulated in order to edify the hearers or readers; whether or not it did in fact edify them will be difficult, if not impossible, to determine.

The question of the intention of a genre, and of particular passages which use that genre, has direct implications for exegesis and interpretation. This question is particularly useful when it helps to distinguish between the intention of the ancient oral material and that of the collector or redactor of that material.

FORM CRITICISM AND OTHER OLD TESTAMENT DISCIPLINES

Form criticism alone is unable to answer all the important questions concerning the Old Testament. It is simply one among many disciplines which must be employed to arrive at an understanding of the literature—and the life—of ancient Israel. A discussion of the relationship between form criticism and other disciplines of Old Testament research will show both the contributions and the limitations of form criticism.

Other Literary Methods. Because form criticism is only one of the means of investigating the *literature* of the Old Testament, it must be used in concert with other methods; specifically literary criticism, tradition criticism and redaction criticism. But the lines between these various methodologies often are difficult to distinguish, and form criticism has influenced significantly these other methods, giving rise to a tendency on the part of some to think of form criticism as a comprehensive approach in which the other disciplines are simply branches.[13] Such an approach has the advantage of taking seriously the continuity of the history of the biblical literature, but the various methods can and should be distinguished from one another for the sake of clarity.

---

13. This tendency is seen in Klaus Koch's very valuable book, *The Growth of the Biblical Tradition,* cf. p. 77.

When Gunkel began his form critical investigations, as we have seen, literary criticism (or source criticism) was the dominant force in biblical scholarship. Literary criticism attempts to answer some very basic and important questions concerning the Old Testament literature: Who was the author (and what were his characteristics), and what is the date (and circumstances) of a certain book or body of material? Literary criticism arrived at the documentary hypothesis concerning the Pentateuch, that is, the conclusion that several writers (identified as J, E, D, P, and others) were responsible for the Pentateuch. It further demonstrated that the prophetic books include material which did not stem from the prophets themselves, or even from their times. It also made great strides in dating the Old Testament writings. These results were accomplished by carefully observing the styles and language of different writers and periods, the inconsistencies, contradictions and duplications in a book (which might indicate multiple authorship), the variations in theological viewpoint, and the historical allusions (which might indicate dates). The continuing validity of literary criticism for exegesis deserves to be emphasized; for one of the very important tasks in the interpretation of ancient literature is determining its date and "authorship."

However, form criticism has had a significant impact on the assumptions, methods and conclusions of literary criticism. It has shown that in many cases one cannot think of the writers as "authors" in the proper sense of the term, but as collectors, editors, or redactors of traditional material. Form criticism has also contributed to the literary critical method new ways of analyzing the work of the writers by looking at the structure, genre and intention, both of what they received and what they wrote. Furthermore, it has shown that what literary critics considered in many cases to be evidence for multiple authorship is in fact evidence for multiple oral traditions used by a redactor.

The primary concern of literary criticism is the literary stage of the material; form criticism, on the other hand, is interested primarily in the recovery and interpretation of the preliterary stage. But form criticism is concerned also with the literary stage itself, for works of literature as well as oral traditions follow genres with conventional structures, settings and intentions.

Other methodologies for investigating the history and meaning of the Old Testament literature have arisen out of form criticism itself. These include tradition criticism and redaction criticism. Tradition criticism (*Überlieferungsgeschichte* or *Traditionsgeschichte*) has been used in various ways. But broadly understood, tradition criticism is an attempt to bring together the results of both source critical and form critical work and provide a complete history of Old Testament literature through its preliterary as well as literary stages. Understood narrowly, however, the term refers only to the history of the *preliterary* development of a body of literature, or to the history of a specific theme or motif.[14] Furthermore, tradition criticism has even been used to refer primarily to the history of the *literary* development of a body of material.[15]

There has been less confusion in the use of the term redaction criticism (*Redactionsgeschichte*). This line of inquiry is concerned with the literary stage of development, with the work and thought of the writers. It is interested in "the theological motivation of an author as this is revealed in the collection, arrangement, editing, and modification of traditional material, and in the composition of new material or the creation of new forms within the traditions. . . ."[16] The term redactor refers to one who has revised oral or literary material. He is not an author, because he did not create something new, but he is more than a collector or editor, for as he revised the material he received, he gave it certain emphases and provided the texts with central themes through his work of composition.[17] We can see, then, the very close relationship between form criticism, source criticism, tradition criticism and redac-

---

14. As in, for example, George W. Coats, *Rebellion in the Wilderness: The Murmuring Motif in the Wilderness Traditions of the Old Testament* (Nashville: Abingdon, 1968).

15. Martin Noth's *Überlieferungsgeschichtliche Studien* (Tübingen: Max Niemeyer, 1943) is concerned with the literary stages of the large Old Testament historical works. His *Überlieferungschichte des Pentateuch* (Stuttgart: W. Kohlhammer, 1948), on the other hand, is primarily concerned with the history of the individual preliterary elements of the Pentateuch and then with the later literary history of the Pentateuch. The latter book is therefore tradition criticism in the broad sense.

16. Norman Perrin, *What Is Redaction Criticism?* (Philadelphia: Fortress, 1969), p. 1.

17. Koch, *The Growth of the Biblical Tradition*, pp. 57–58.

tion criticism. All of these methods must be employed to understand the full history of the Old Testament literature.

The Work of the Historian. The historian cannot begin his task of reconstructing the events of the past without a firm grasp of the sources for that reconstruction. The major source for the history of ancient Israel is the Old Testament itself. To be sure, the historian has other evidence at his disposal, including the material remains unearthed by archaeology and the written materials recovered from other ancient Near Eastern civilizations. But one who studies the history of ancient Israel—including the history of Israel's religion—must employ all the literary methodologies at his disposal to analyze, interpret and evaluate his main body of evidence, the Old Testament.

Form criticism, along with the other literary disciplines, has made and continues to make specific contributions to the work of the historian. It is useful as a critical aid in evaluating the historian's sources. Merely the identification of material according to genre helps one judge its historical usefulness. A text which is recognized to be a more or less neutral record (such as a king list or a list of tribal claims), contemporary with the events it describes, will contain more reliable information than a later theologically motivated saga which claims to deal with the same events. Historiography (such as 2 Sam. 9–20, 1 Kings 1–2) is more useful than prophetic legends. The results of such analysis often are taken to be entirely negative (and in certain cases they are, in the sense that the historical reliability of some material has been called into question). But such an analysis can lead to a positive reassessment of materials of all types: Sagas usually tell us more about the life and time of the period in which they were circulated and written down than they do about the events they mean to describe. A careful form critical and traditio-historical analysis, however, can help the historian to distinguish between the old and the new and the historically reliable and the unreliable in those sagas. It also helps us to separate older traditions from newer interpretations.

Form criticism is also a tool of historical reconstruction itself. Along with traditio-historical research it helps uncover the ancient traditions within later written documents, often pushing the sources back closer to the events they describe. Through the recovery of the ancient settings of the genres, the form critic helps to reconstruct the institutions, customs and events of those settings themselves. Many details of the procedure of the Israelite law court, for example, have been recovered through the form critical analysis of the formulas and genres used in that procedure.

The Work of the Old Testament Theologian. Whatever else the biblical theologian does, he must base his work on an understanding of the thought of the Old Testament, and that understanding must be based on a critical and careful assessment—including a form critical analysis—of the Old Testament literature. Genres of speech and literature are shaped not only by a people's institutions and customs, but also by their theology. A study of those genres sheds light on that theology. It is not by accident that the distinctive and prevalent genre for theological expression among Israel's neighbors was the myth. And it is not by accident that Israel spoke of God by describing what he had done in the life of the nation in historic events. Different genres reflect different world views. The rise of historiography, in the proper sense of the term, stemmed from a certain conception of man and his past. In order fully to understand the thought of the Old Testament, then, one must examine not only what is said, but *how* it is said.

Form criticism furthermore, with tradition criticism and redaction criticism, enables us to separate and therefore hear the voices of many traditions within a given text or texts. The theologian can then come to recognize in those texts not simply one witness, but many. He can hear the assertions and proclamations of the many generations which created and handed on and reinterpreted these traditions.

The discovery of the settings of the genres and of specific texts brings flesh and blood to the bones of the text: these ancient genres and texts spring from every facet of the lives of the people of Israel. And the discovery of the ancient intentions of the genres and of specific texts enables the interpreter to see how those ancient texts can function kerygmatically once again in contemporary situations.

21

II.
Form Criticism at Work: Some Representative Genres and Texts

The Old Testament contains a rich collection of literary and oral genres of all kinds. Several factors account for the richness and diversity of this collection. First, because the development of the Old Testament spanned several centuries it preserves genres which arose from different social and political structures. Some stories and songs arose from the life of the seminomadic tribes, others from the early Israelite tribal league, others from the institutions of the monarchy, others from the postexilic religious community. This long history also helps to explain the influence upon Israelite literature from Canaanite, Egyptian, and Mesopotamian sources. (But in view of Israel's location near the crossroads of the civilizations of the ancient world and her relatively weak political and cultural position, it is surprising that the influence was not even more significant!)

Second, the Old Testament preserves the traditions of the people of Israel as a whole, and not just the works of a few creative individual writers. While it does contain literary inventions in the proper sense of the term, it also transmits to us the folk "literature"—stories, songs, sayings, records, etc.— of a people. No comparable collection of literature and lore exists from any Western people.

Third, one must not ignore the influence of the particular religious beliefs and practices of ancient Israel upon the nature of this collection of literature. This is to say more than to point out the obvious fact that the Old Testament is, for the most part, religious literature. Ancient Israel apparently did not make the same kind of distinctions between "religious" and "secular" which we are accustomed to make. To be sure, Israel was aware of a distinction between holy and profane; that awareness apparently grew stronger as years went on. But in ancient Israel, no sphere of life was exempt from the will of Israel's God. Thus Israel's faith comes to expression not only in a special religious language such as creeds and hymns, but in genres of all kinds. What may appear to be an innocent and entertaining story becomes a vehicle for the expression of that faith. Even the wisdom literature which is founded on a very "secular" understanding of the world eventually is brought under the rubric of the law of the Lord.

As a result of these facts, the pages of the Old Testament are filled with genres of literature and speech which arose from every facet of the life of ancient Israel, from the elevated lyric poetry of the most serious religious ceremonies to the most mundane genres from everyday life, such as drinking songs or arguments.

We could not possibly discuss all of these genres here. To do so would require a work of many hundred pages. Furthermore, one may seriously doubt whether the study of these ancient genres has progressed to the point where such a catalog is possible. Nor is such a catalog necessarily desirable. It might convey the impression that the goal of form criticism is simply to find the most appropriate classification, the proper pigeon-hole or label for each Old Testament text. This is by no means the case. One must, to be sure, develop an awareness of the extent and nature of the distinctive Old Testament genres. But the proper goal of form criticism is to find the relationship of the text to life at the various stages of its history; all generalizing and cataloging should serve that purpose. Becoming accustomed to asking the appropriate form critical questions is far more important than learning the types themselves. Our aim here is to show how these questions may be applied to some representative Old Testament genres. Then when one turns to other Old Testament texts he may be better able to see the relationship between that text and the life of ancient Israel.

At almost every point we shall be acknowledging our debt to the work of Hermann Gunkel. We have noted above that it was Gunkel who first applied the methods of form criticism to the biblical literature, and that he listed and described the main genres of the Old Testament. He also produced extensive and detailed investigations of the narratives[1] and the cultic poetry.[2] Since the first decades of the twentieth century, Gunkel's methods and conclusions have been extended, refined, challenged, and—in some cases—even abandoned. But his work still remains our point of departure.

His concise summary of the main literary genres of the Old Testament has not been superceded:

There is first the broad classification into Prose and Poetry. Narrative is usually found in prose form, and the following different kinds of narrative can be distinguished: stories about the deities, i.e. Myths; primitive Folk-tales (of these two, only fragments are found in Israel); the popular Saga; the longer Romance; the religious Legend; and, lastly, Historical Narrative in the stricter sense. Poetical literary types include: the oracular wisdom, the prophetic oracular saying, the Lyric—the two last mentioned being especially frequent. Lyric poetry is again subdivided into (a) secular lyrics, such as the Dirge, the Love song, the scornful lay, the song of carouse, the wedding song, the song of victory, the royal song, and (b) spiritual lyrics, including the Hymn, the Thanksgiving, the Dirge (both private and public), the Eschatological Psalm, etc. Numerous types are found conjoined in the prophetic writings—the Vision in narrative form, the Prophetic Oracle, the Discourse (in many forms). Among these last mentioned the oldest is that which foretells the future, and may either be the Threat or the Promise; the Invective, upbraiding sin; the Exhortation, calling to well-doing, and many others.[3]

Throughout the work which follows we shall be returning to Gunkel's categories, describing them more fully, showing how they have been refined or changed since his time, and above all, attempting to show the place and use of some of the main genres in the life of ancient Israel.

It will not be possible—nor even desirable—to confine ourselves exclusively to form critical study. Form criticism can-

1. Hermann Gunkel, *Genesis, übersetzt und erklärt.*
2. Hermann Gunkel and Joachim Begrich, *Einleitung in die Psalmen.*
3. Hermann Gunkel, "Fundamental Problems of Hebrew Literary History," in *What Remains of the Old Testament*, pp. 59–60.

not be carried on in a vacuum. We must and shall depend upon the conclusions of source critical work,[4] and the form critical work should help to place each text into the history of its redaction. We shall not refrain entirely from commenting on the implications for the historian of the form critical investigations. Finally, we shall try to learn something of the theological assumptions and implications of our text, for, after all, most of the genres of the Old Testament mean to speak in one way or another of the relationship between God and man.

NARRATIVE GENRES

A narrative simply tells a story. Usually it includes at least a setting (where the events occurred), a plot (or at least a tension and the resolution of that tension), and characterization of the actors. Within this broad definition many variations are possible: the setting may be real or imagined, in this world or another (for example, the realm of the gods); the plot may be simple or complex, encompassing many years or a few minutes; and the characters may be few or many, described in minute detail externally and/or internally, or only briefly noted. On the basis of the manner in which the main characteristics are developed, one determines which particular narrative genre he is dealing with, learns something of the setting which gave rise to that genre, and gains insight into the intentions of the particular example.

For very good theological reasons narratives were especially significant in ancient Israel. Israel's most distinctive way of speaking of God was just to tell the story of her life with her God. This is so because in ancient Israel there was a deep awareness of the historical drama, based on the assumption that this drama has ultimate significance. Or, to put it another way, to the ancient Israelite, God acts in history and is encountered in the ongoing affairs of men. So, instead of generalizing about the nature or being of God, ancient Israel tended simply to tell the story of God's acts.

---

4. Most form critics, from Gunkel to the present day, have continued to base their work upon source critical analysis. This is in contrast to the tendencies of the "oral tradition" school, as exemplified in the words of Ivan Engnell: "The traditio-historical critic must completely do away with the anachronistic book-view of the literary-historical method." Engnell, *A Rigid Scrutiny: Critical Essays on the Old Testament,* trans. and ed. John T. Willis (Nashville: Vanderbilt University Press, 1969), p. 11.

However, this story was told only in certain ways. Not all possible narrative genres are found in the Old Testament, and some are found only rarely or in remnants. Myths and fairy tales, for example, are rare or nonexistent. Heroic tales are scarce. Saga, legend and history predominate. These facts can hardly be considered accidental; we shall attempt to account for them below. First, however, we should define and describe the main narrative genres of the Old Testament.

The definitions of the major narrative genres as established by Gunkel more than sixty years ago remain the basis for most general introductions and commentaries on the narrative books of the Old Testament.[5] However, there have been some significant developments in recent years, and a great deal of work remains to be done. Few scholars are entirely satisfied with the terminology which must be employed, but we must use what we have until a better understanding is developed.

The main narrative genres to be considered as one examines the Old Testament are the following: the myth, the folktale (fairy tales and fables), the saga, the legend, the novelette, and historical narratives in the strict sense.[6] Gunkel designated all of these except history as "poetic narratives." He did not mean to imply of course, that the poetic narratives necessarily employ meter or rhyme. The distinction was drawn not only on the basis of structure (form), but also in terms of different intentions and settings: "History, which claims to inform us of what has actually happened, is in its very nature prose, while legend [better, "saga" for the German *Sage*] is by nature poetry, its aim is to please, to elevate, to inspire, and to move."[7] Such narratives, then, are not poetry in the narrow sense; they are poetic.

Myths and Folktales

The first types to be considered are myths and folktales. According to the simplest definition, which has been used

---

5. Gunkel, *Genesis*. The introduction to this commentary has been translated and published as *The Legends of Genesis*.

6. Cf. especially Hermann Gunkel, "Die israelitische Literatur," in *Die Kultur der Gegenwart*, 1. 7, pp. 15 ff.

7. Gunkel, *The Legends of Genesis*, p. 10.

widely since the time of the Grimm brothers, myths are stories of the gods. If we accept this definition—and it is useful, indeed basic to any understanding of the literary genre—then we must agree with Gunkel that there are not myths as such in the Old Testament, only "faded myths."[8] Since the religion of Israel had room for only one god, and since stories require more than one character, ancient Israel had no use for myths in the strict sense of the term.

But myth is a very problematical term. It has been used freely not only by students of literature and folklore, but by theologians and philosophers as well, and defined both narrowly and broadly. Even if we attempt to confine ourselves strictly to descriptions of the literary phenomena which we characterize as myths, we shall want to learn something of the particular point of view which is assumed by such stories. The most obvious assumption behind myth is polytheism. It is clear that the mainstream of Israelite thought as reflected in the Old Testament was not polytheistic, but it is equally clear that a great many mythological motifs are in fact preserved in the Old Testament. In order to understand these motifs and the nature of this borrowing, we must deepen our definition of myth.

One very productive attempt to understand the view of reality behind myth and to apply that understanding to the Old Testament is the work of Brevard S. Childs.[9] Childs goes beyond the narrow form critical definition to an understanding of myth as a phenomenon in religion: "Myth is a form by which the existing structure of reality is understood and maintained. It concerns itself with showing how an action of a deity, conceived of as occurring in the primeval world order is maintained through the actualization of the myth in the cult."[10] Since in the cultures which surrounded ancient Israel myth was the dominant form of religious expression, it was inevitable that some mythical material would be appropriated by Old Testament traditions. But because of her own understanding

---

8. Cf. ibid., p. 14.
9. Brevard S. Childs, *Myth and Reality in the Old Testament*, SBT 27 (London: SCM, 1960).
10. Ibid., p. 29.

of reality, ancient Israel did not simply imitate mythical forms of expression nor appropriate them without—in most cases—some radical transformations. Childs has shown that mythical motifs are present at many points in the Old Testament (he examines in detail some of the key passages) but that these motifs never are appropriated without tension. For example, Genesis 1:1–2 reflects to a certain extent the mythical motif of the creation of the world in terms of a conflict between the gods, but the writer of this chapter has broken the myth without fully destroying it. The biblical writer employed some of the mythical tradition, but he used it to testify to the sovereignty of God who made all things.[11]

Genesis 3:1–5 employs the mythical theme of the evil demon in the form of a snake hostile to both God and man.[12] But in the story of the Fall, the serpent is simply one of God's creatures; the biblical writer has used the motif to comment on the nature of sin. "Evil is not created by God nor is it outside God's power; nevertheless, sin is an active power, a demonic force. It is an incomprehensible hatred for God which revolts against his authority."[13] Other passages in which mythological themes are adapted to serve the biblical faith are Genesis 6:1–4 (the account of the marriage of the "sons of gods" and the daughters of men), Exodus 4:24–26 (the story of an attempt on the life of Moses by what is apparently a nocturnal demon), Isaiah 11:6–9 (which employs the myth of paradise), Isaiah 14:12–21 (which uses mythological motifs in a taunt psalm concerning the fall of the king of Babylon), and many others.[14]

From the study of the Old Testment use of mythological motifs in the light of Near Eastern mythology, it becomes clear that myth presupposes not only a polytheistic religion, but also certain ideas of time and space. Israel appropriated and used and changed not only certain mythical motifs, but also these mythical views of reality. However, "the broken myth within Israel's tradition cannot be judged merely negatively as part of a primitive stage in development, but it served a

---

11. Ibid., esp. p. 42.
12. Ibid., p. 47; cf. Gunkel, *Genesis*, p. 15.
13. Childs, *Myth and Reality in the Old Testament*, pp. 47–48.
14. On these passages cf. Childs, *Myth and Reality in the Old Testament*.

unique purpose in communicating the biblical understanding of reality."[15]

Similar conclusions are reached by Bernhard W. Anderson in his study of the mythical motifs of creation and chaos in the Old Testament. He shows "how the biblical writers appropriated the motif of the conflict between the Creator and the powers of chaos from the religions of the ancient Near East; they radically reinterpreted the motif, however, so that it is now used poetically in the Scriptures to express a dramatic conflict in which man's existence is at stake. In the biblical perspective . . . man finds who he is and what life really means, not in relation to nature, with its cycles of death and renewal, but in relation to history where God calls him to a historical task."[16]

The Old Testament use of fairy tales and fables is similar to its treatment of myths. It preserves few, if any, complete fairy tales or fables, but ancient Israel certainly knew such stories, and a great many motifs from folktales have found their way into the Old Testament.[17] Fables, which personify animals or plants in order to teach or to entertain, are represented in the story of the thistle of Lebanon which sent to the cedar of Lebanon asking for its daughter as a wife (2 Kings 14:9 ff.), Jotham's fable (Judges 9:8–15), and a great many more or less poetic uses of such motifs. Fairy tales, which assume ideas of magical causation, are reflected in many stories, including the tale of Jonah, the stories of Elijah, and even the story of Moses' "magical" staff.

Saga

The saga is clearly one of the most common narrative genres in the Old Testament.[18] According to Gunkel, sagas deal with

---

15. Ibid., p. 95.
16. Bernhard W. Anderson, *Creation Versus Chaos: The Reinterpretation of Mythical Symbolism in the Bible* (New York: Association, 1967), p. 8.
17. See esp. Hermann Gunkel, *Das Märchen im Alten Testament* (Tübingen: Mohr [Siebeck], 1921).
18. Some confusion was introduced into the study of this genre by the mistranslation of the German term *Sage* as "legend" in the translation of Gunkel's introduction to Genesis, *Die Sagen der Genesis*. In the discussion which follows we shall read "saga" for the German *Sage*. For a discussion of the difference between saga and legend, and of the nature of the genre legend, see below pp. 38 ff.

the affairs of men while myths deal with the affairs of the gods. However, Gunkel's more detailed description of the characteristics of Old Testament saga is spelled out by comparing saga with history. Saga originates at the oral level and depends partly upon tradition and partly upon imagination. History usually is found in written form since it assumes a sort of scientific activity. History deals with public occurrences, while saga deals with personal and private matters. When saga deals with political affairs and public individuals they are treated in such a way as to attract popular attention; that is, it is more interested in their private lives than their public lives. Saga frequently reports things which are incredible, while history reports the credible. Saga may speak of the direct intervention of God in the affairs of man, but when history speaks of God it is only as the last and ultimate cause of everything.[19]

The Book of Genesis, Gunkel concluded, is for the most part a collection of sagas. Originally they existed independently; each one comprised a complete whole. Only later were the individual sagas compiled and finally written down.[20] One of the primary characteristics, then, of the saga is its brevity. Each is "filled with a single harmonious sentiment."[21] A saga treats only a very small number of characters, and makes a clear distinction between the major and minor actors. Characters tend to be presented as types rather than as individuals, and little or no development of character is shown.[22] Furthermore the characters "often fail to speak where the modern writer would surely have them do so, and where the very nature of the case seems to require it."[23]

As a rule characterization is subordinated to the action in the story. There is more interest in outward objective facts than in the inner life of man. The stories are simple, but not self-evident from the first words. Simplicity is achieved by the arrangement of the story into parts, usually as a number of little scenes.[24] The sagas in Genesis—and those in the Old

---

19. Gunkel, *The Legends of Genesis*, pp. 3-8.
20. Ibid., pp. 42-43.
21. Ibid., p. 44.
22. Ibid., pp. 52-56.
23. Ibid., p. 63.
24. Ibid., pp. 50, 57-61, 69 ff.

Testament as a whole—refrain from giving detailed descriptions of the settings of the stories. There is no intimate feeling for the landscape. (Gunkel concluded from this fact that there is no love of nature in Genesis.)[25]

On the basis of both form and content, Gunkel distinguished the sagas in Genesis 1–11 from those in Genesis 12–50. The former are concerned with the origin of the world and of the progenitors of the human race; their locality is remote and their sphere of interest the whole world. In them the action of the divinity is more direct and immediate; they have a decidedly "mythical" character: for the most part they are "faded myths."[26] The latter are the sagas of the patriarchs of Israel; they take place in the well-known places in Canaan and adjacent lands.[27]

Gunkel noted in the stories of the patriarchs several different kinds of saga. Those which reflect historical occurrences, such as the migrations of tribes and the establishment of treaties, he classified as *historical*. Those which focused upon descriptions of race and tribal relations, such as the stories of Jacob and Esau, he designated *ethnographic*, suggesting that in many cases the stories which talk about the ancestors mean to talk about tribes. But he classified a great many of the sagas in Genesis—and elsewhere in the Old Testament—as etiological, that is, they were written in order to explain the origin of something. He assumed the picture of the child who observes the world around him and asks: Why? Primitive peoples, he suggested, ask questions about the world and produce answers which, though incorrect, are interesting. He classified the various etiological sagas according to the kinds of questions they seemed to answer.

There are, first of all, ethnological etiologies, that is, sagas which give the reasons for the relations between tribes. These stories tell how the various patriarchs, and therefore their descendants, received particular lands. Present relationships usually are explained in terms of some action by the patriarchs in the past. Second, there are etymological etiologies, stories

---

25. Ibid., pp. 67 ff.
26. Ibid., pp. 13–14.
27. Ibid., p. 13.

which explain the origin of names, and purport to give the real meaning of those names. These etymologies are founded on the idea that the name of a thing is deeply related to its reality. But as a rule the etiology is not scientifically correct; often it is based simply upon the sounds of words. For example, Beersheba is explained both as the "well of seven," and the "well of the oath," because there is some similarity between both these explanations and the name itself. Third, there are ceremonial or cultic etiologies which attempt to explain the origin of important religious practices. They may explain the sacredness of a given holy place, or important rites such as circumcision or the celebration of the Passover. Fourth, there are what Gunkel called geological etiologies. Such stories explain the origin of a locality or a geological formation, for example the Dead Sea or even a pillar of salt. Finally, there are "mixed sagas" in which various types are combined. The story of the flight of Hagar (Genesis 16) is ethnographic because it deals with the life of Ishmael, it is an ethnological etiology because it tries to explain certain features of tribal life, and it is an explanation of the holiness of a place; it also is etymological in that it explains the names of Ishmael and Lacharoy.[28]

Gunkel based these classifications upon what he considered the chief or dominant features of each. "Along with these go the purely ornamental or aesthetic features, twining about the others like vines over their trellises."[29]

The question which must be raised at this point is whether or not Gunkel in fact based his classifications of saga upon the dominant or central features of each story. Some serious questions have been raised about these classifications in recent years.

First of all, there have been some significant developments in the study of the problem of etiology in the Old Testament.[30]

---

28. Ibid., pp. 19–35.
29. Ibid., p. 36.
30. We are not raising here the much-debated question of the historical worth of the stories which have been classified as etiologies. Historians of ancient Israel have been divided on this point in recent years. For some history of this discussion and one point of view, cf. especially John Bright, *Early Israel in Recent History Writing*, SBT 19 (London: SCM, 1956).

Some have insisted that the etiological elements of most Old Testament narratives are secondary, that is, either they are of secondary importance in the story or they were secondarily added by later editors. Most of the recent form critical work has focused on the problem of identifying the "marks" of etiological narrative.[31] Burke O. Long has examined some of the phrases which were commonly taken to be etiological formulas, such as the etymological etiology at the conclusion of the story of the tower of Babel: "Therefore its name was called Babel, because there the Lord confused the language of all the earth; and from there the Lord scattered them abroad over the face of all the earth" (Gen. 11:9). He concludes that only rarely are any of the formulas related to a "story" complex; thus seldom can these marks of the etiology be used to determine whether or not a narrative served an etiological purpose. In a few cases the relationship between the etiological formula and the story is functional—that is, the formula is a constitutive part of the story—but this relationship is confined almost exclusively to very short narratives. "Thus great caution is demanded in speaking of *etymological etiological narrative*. An example of such is quite rare."[32] Similarly, Brevard S. Childs has shown that the formula "until this day," which often occurs with the explanation of the origin of something, seldom has a truly etiological function, but "in the great majority of cases is a formula of personal testimony added to, and confirming, a received tradition."[33] It thus becomes clear that the influence of etiological motifs has been exaggerated and that Gunkel's interpretation of sagas in Genesis needs serious reexamination. Seldom is the etiological function the chief or dominant feature by which Gunkel sought to classify the stories.

What is required now is a broader approach to the problem,

---

31. See especially Burke O. Long, *The Problem of Etiological Narrative in the Old Testament*, BZAW 108 (Berlin: Töpelmann, 1968); Brevard S. Childs, "A Study of the Formula 'until this day,' " *JBL* 82 (1963): 279–92; Jerry Fichtner, "Die etymologische Ätiologie in der Namengebung der geschichtlichen Bücher des Alten Testaments," *VT* 6 (1956): 372–96.

32. Long, *The Problem of Etiological Narrative in the Old Testament*, p. 56.

33. Childs, "A Study of the Formula 'until this day,' " p. 292.

one which will attempt to determine the marks (not only in terms of formulas but also in terms of structure) which reveal a story's function. Furthermore, such questions need to be raised in the light of the history of the tradition of a given story; by adding an etiological formula at the conclusion of a story a later redactor may have altered the function of the original story, making into an etiology what originally was something else. The pursuit of these questions should eventually result in a new understanding of Israelite narrative genres in general, an understanding which will assist the historian as he evaluates the reliability of his sources and the theologian as he interprets the documents from Israel's faith.

From another perspective Claus Westermann has called into question the adequacy of Gunkel's term *saga* for the stories in the Old Testament, specifically those in Genesis.[34] He points out that the term saga is traditionally and firmly associated with hero sagas, in which the most important motif is the attempt to accomplish great deeds and thus to gain honor. It is quite clear, as he points out, that the narratives in Genesis are not hero sagas. Indeed, there are no such sagas in the entire Old Testament (though the stories of the judges come close).[35] Westermann prefers to call the stories in Genesis 11–50 "family narratives." Such stories, which are found in the traditions of other cultures, arose in the period when the family and the tribe were the dominant social institutions. The themes are the family relationships among the ancestors: in the Abraham cycle (Gen. 25–36) it is the parent-child relationship; in the Jacob-Esau cycle (Gen. 25–36) the relationship between brother and brother; in the Joseph cycle the complicated events which occur between the father, a brother, and the circle of brothers.[36] On the other hand the stories in Genesis 1–11 deal with events long ago and far away. Their setting is not the family but the wide wide world. Westermann identifies these as narratives of guilt and punishment.[37]

---

34. Claus Westermann, "Arten der Erzählungen in der Genesis," in *Forschung am Alten Testament*, pp. 9–91.
35. Ibid., p. 39.
36. Ibid., p. 38. Cf. also pp. 36 ff., 39, 89 ff.
37. Ibid., pp. 47 ff.

Westermann's reservations concerning the use of the term saga for the Old Testament stories are well founded. There are significant differences between the Old Testament narratives and the Norse sagas or even the epic sagas of the ancient Near East, such as the story of Gilgamesh. However, the term *family narrative* is hardly an adequate description of the stories in Genesis. It is too broad to be very useful. Thus it seems best to continue to use the term saga while at the same time attempting to determine what is distinctive and characteristic about the sagas of the Old Testament.

All peoples shape their literary traditions according to their institutions and beliefs. When we begin to look for what is distinctive about the literature of the Old Testament we are confronted immediately not only with the specific historical events and circumstances of ancient Israel but also with her faith: "In Ancient Israel the principal power in the forming of saga was faith. In any case, we do not have a single saga that has not received from faith its decisive stamp and orientation. In every instance the degree of this revision, stamp, and orientation is completely different."[38] Consequently the patriarchal sagas, for example, are not concerned with the great deeds of heroes, but with the activity of God.[39]

History

The Old Testament includes narrative works which, for want of a better term, we must classify as history.[40] Some of the main features of this genre, as understood by Gunkel, have been noted above: History originates as written literature, presupposes a kind of scientific activity, and deals with public events. It is a more or less systematic written account of events, especially those which affect nations and institutions. But history does not simply record, it also seeks to explain the meaning of the events, usually in terms of cause and effect.

---

38. Gerhard von Rad, *Genesis: A Commentary*, trans. John H. Marks (Philadelphia: Westminster, 1961), p. 35.

39. Cf. ibid., p. 36.

40. "History" is used here in reference to the literary genre, not the reality which the genre means to describe. Perhaps we should capitulate to the popular usage which equates "history" with "the past," and therefore use the term "historiography" or "history writing." But such a careless use of the term "history" has caused more harm than good. There is a literary genre and a scholarly discipline for which "history" is the proper term.

The historian wants to make sense of the past, so he writes a coherent and cohesive narrative of events, the meaning of which he interprets either explicitly or implicitly by means of his selection and organization. A simple list of events or an uncritical record cannot be classified as history.

To be sure, the Old Testament contains no historical writing in the modern sense of the term. Since the Enlightenment history has been seen as a strictly humanistic and scientific discipline. According to R. G. Collingwood, history is research or inquiry which attempts to answer questions, its object is the actions of human beings in the past, it proceeds by interpreting evidence, and its purpose is human self-knowledge, that is, it attempts to learn what man is by discovering what man has done.[41] In particular the line between history and saga often is difficult to discern in works from antiquity. Early historians—including both those of ancient Israel and such writers as Herodotus and Livy—often used as sources not only reliable historical documents but also sagas and legends. Nevertheless, "history," or perhaps popular history or theocratic history, remains the best term to describe some of the documents of the Old Testament.

Certainly the best example of the genre in the Old Testament is the throne succession history of David (2 Sam. 9–20, 1 Kings 1–2). This document is Israelite history writing at its very best. As a result of this writer's historical scholarship, the last part of the reign of David is one of the best documented periods in the history of Israel. The author, who must have written his work during the reign of Solomon, had access to firsthand information about David, but he was not content to simply give a list of events. He worked his data into a consistent whole, painting a picture which not only describes but also interprets the events in terms of causes and effects. The work is a finely styled narrative, with the drama of a tragedy and the detailed reporting of historical events. He draws his characters as individuals and not types, and is sensitive to their feelings and motives. From what must have been a wealth of information about the period at his disposal he has selected the data which he considered relevant and organized it thematically.

---

41. R. G. Collingwood, *The Idea of History* (New York: Oxford Univ. Press, 1946), pp. 9 ff.

Two themes run through the history. The first deals with the question of the successor to David on the throne of Israel. One by one the possible claimants are dealt with until finally the crown rests on a very unlikely head. It is clear that one of the historian's major purposes was to explain why Solomon instead of one of the more logical successors came to the throne after the death of David. The second theme which runs through the material is that of the figure of David himself, specifically the declining years of the great king. The story begins when David has made his major accomplishments and is secure in Jerusalem in control of a vast empire. But the turning point in David's life is described in 2 Samuel 11, David's affair with Bathsheba and his murder of her husband. In subtle ways the historian shows how the blessing turns to curse for David and "the sword does not depart from his house." The writer obviously believes that all of David's troubles are the result of his sin against Uriah the Hittite. But he tells the story in such a way that it is understandable and credible even to those who do not share his belief in the relationship between sin and punishment. Given David's personality, the personalities of the figures around him, and the situations which developed, it appears almost inevitable to the reader that the old king would lose the strength which brought him to the throne in the first place.

The court historian obviously believed that God acts in history, but he describes no miracles, no direct interventions in history by God. He confines himself almost entirely to the description of human affairs. There is a decidedly "secular"— almost humanistic—atmosphere about his work. Only rarely does he speak explicitly of God, and when he does we can see that he has stepped back from the narrative and passed judgment on the events. One such comment is directly related to the theme of the throne succession, indeed explains why Solomon came to the throne: "And the Lord loved him [Solomon]" (2 Sam. 12:24). Another serves essentially the same function in the theme of David's decline. After telling the story of David's sin against Uriah, the narrator comments: "But the thing that David had done displeased the Lord" (2 Sam. 11:27). Thus while the account does not meet the strict requirements for modern historiography as described by Collingwood, it does fit the description given by Gunkel (cf. above, p. 30). Without a doubt this document is one of the milestones in the history of the development of the genre and indeed of the discipline of history itself.

Legend and Novelette

Many other narrative genres are represented in the Old Testament. Two of them should be noted here: the legend and the novelette. No commonly accepted definition of legend has appeared. The line between legend and saga in particular is difficult to establish. The term *legend* often is used quite loosely—sometimes as a synonym for saga—to refer to unverified traditions about the past.[42] Legend and saga do have much in common. Both are poetic narrative genres, and more often than not the traditions which they transmit cannot be verified.

However, one can and should distinguish between the two. (There are, for example, basic difference in tone and intention between the *legends* of Elisha in 2 Kings 2–7 and the stories of Jacob, most of which are sagas.) While a fuller understanding of these genres must await more detailed analysis of the Old Testament narratives—especially in the light of ancient Near Eastern parallels—some basic distinctions may be suggested here. The legend is the product of a more highly developed literary consciousness, and is decidedly more "spiritual" in tone than the saga. Legends ordinarily deal either with holy men, holy places, or religious ceremonies. The pattern for the understanding of legend usually is found in the lives of the Christian saints, such as the *Acta Martyrum* or the *Acta Sanctorum*.[43] Legends of the lives and deeds of holy men tend to glorify those men and often present them as examples for later generations. Legends of sacred places and religious ceremonies usually explain and justify the sacredness of the

---

42. The two major introductions to the Old Testament illustrate the confusion. Eissfeldt distinguishes between saga and legend (*The Old Testament: An Introduction*, trans. Peter R. Ackroyd [New York: Harper & Row, 1965], pp. 38–47) while Fohrer considers the various types of legends and sagas together (*Introduction to the Old Testament*, trans. David E. Green [Nashville: Abingdon, 1968], pp. 90–95).
43. Cf. Andre Jolles, *Einfache Formen* (1930; reprint ed., Tübingen: Max Niemeyer, 1958), pp. 23 ff.

place or the religious practice in terms of some miraculous occurrence or historical event.

There are relatively few Old Testament stories which may be called legends of holy men in the strict sense of the term, for the same reason that there is little biography in the Old Testament. Ancient Israel was less concerned with special individuals than with the special and sacred history of the people of God. But there are some legends in the strict sense, and a great many legendary elements in other stories.

Some of the best examples of prophetic legends are found in the traditions about Elisha. In 2 Kings 2–7 we find a number of stories, most of them anecdotal in length, united around the theme of the miraculous power of Elisha. In the stories of the prophet's parting of the waters of the Jordan (2 Kings 2:13–14), the story of the widow's jar of oil (2 Kings 4:1–8), the stories of Elisha's miraculous help of the Shunamite woman (2 Kings 4:8–37), and the healing of the leprosy of Naaman (2 Kings 5:1–19) we recognize the voice of the pious followers of Elisha. These legends do not simply boast of the power of Elisha, but mean to bear witness to the power of Israel's God expressed through the prophet. This is a typical intention of the spiritual legend of a great man. Other legends or legendary motifs attached to human personalities are the stories of Sampson (Judges 13–16) and the account of David's battle with the giant Goliath (1 Sam. 17).

Examples of legends of holy places and religious institutions are the stories of the miraculous power of the ark (1 Sam. 4–6), the account of David's establishment of a place for the ark in Jerusalem (2 Sam. 6:1–19), and the explanation of the altar at Ophrah (Judges 6:11–24).

The novel is a modern Western art form which had its beginnings in the eighteenth century with the works of Daniel Defoe and Henry Fielding and came into prominence in the nineteenth century with the works of Sir Walter Scott. The novel is an art form; that is, it is the work of a writer and not the product of tradition. But it has been called the loosest of all art forms. At the very least it is a long fictitious prose narrative which presents characters in a plot. Such stories are not found before the eighteenth century, but the forerunner of

39

the novel is the novella, for example, the *Decameron* of Boccaccio. Novellas are short fictitious stories with a plot and usually also a point.

Some Old Testament stories bear many of the characteristics of the novella. The best example is the Joseph story, Genesis 37, 39–47, and 50. The story is not an entirely new invention by a creative writer; rather, old traditions, for the most part saga, have been combined artistically and creatively into a work of art. Whereas the stories of Abraham, Isaac and Jacob consist of collections of independent little stories which can be separated from one another, the story of Joseph is a well-organized literary document. It bears more affinity to the novella than it does to the saga. There is a plot with a clear development, a climax and a denouement, and many little subplots as well. The movement from scene to scene is effected with good transitions. The point of view is clearly more sophisticated than that in the other stories in Genesis. For example, now when foreigners speak to one another they use interpreters, while Abraham could speak quite directly to anyone. There is a definite anthropological interest, and few explicit cultic or theological concerns. The writer is especially interested in the psychological dimension of his characters, not hesitating to describe their emotional reactions in detail. Above all, the writer portrays his characters as real human beings who change and develop over the years. At the beginning of the story Joseph is a young man, the favorite of his father, and something of a spoiled brat. But in the end he is a mature, sensitive and sophisticated man. When his brothers and his father appear before him in the Egyptian court they are all mellow with age and experience. One can almost see them bent under the burden of the famine.[44]

No direct appearances by God are mentioned, but one can see that God is at work on the human heart. The point of view then is similar to that in the court history of David: God works in history through indirect means. When we arrive at the end of the story we can see the point of all the events. In the final scene, when Joseph's brothers beg forgiveness for

---

44. Cf. Gerhard von Rad, "The Joseph Narrative and Ancient Wisdom," in *The Problem of the Hexateuch and Other Essays*, trans. E. W. Trueman Dicken (Edinburgh: Oliver & Boyd, Ltd., 1966), pp. 292 ff.

40

the treachery in their youth, Joseph replies, "As for you, you meant evil against me; but God meant it for good, to bring it about that many people should be kept alive as they are today" (Gen. 50:20). This, finally, is the point of the story: the relationship between God's work and human purposes is a mystery.[45] The point of view of the writer is very similar to that expressed in early wisdom sayings: "A man's mind plans his way, but Yahweh directs his steps" (Prov. 16:9). It is not surprising that a sophisticated literary consciousness developed in the circles of educated wisdom writers.[46]

An Example: Jacob's Struggle at the Jabbok (Gen. 32:22–32)

[22]The same night he arose and took his two wives, his two maids, and his eleven children, and crossed the ford of the Jabbok. [23]He took them and sent them across the stream, and likewise everything that he had. [24]And Jacob was left alone; and a man wrestled with him until the breaking of the day. [25]When the man saw that he did not prevail against Jacob, he touched the hollow of his thigh; and Jacob's thigh was put out of joint as he wrestled with him. [26]Then he said, "Let me go, for the day is breaking." But Jacob said, "I will not let you go, unless you bless me." [27]And he said to him, "What is your name?" And he said, "Jacob." [28]Then he said, "Your name shall no more be called Jacob, but Israel, for you have striven with God and with men, and have prevailed." [29]Then Jacob asked him, "Tell me, I pray, your name." But he said, "Why is it that you ask my name?" And there he blessed him. [30]So Jacob called the name of the place Peniel, saying, "For I have seen God face to face, and yet my life is preserved." [31]The sun rose upon him as he passed Penuel, limping because of his thigh. [32]Therefore to this day the Israelites do not eat the sinew of the hip which is upon the hollow of the thigh, because he touched the hollow of Jacob's thigh on the sinew of the hip.

The story of Jacob's struggle at the Jabbok does not offer a simple test for form critical analysis; it is a complicated and

45. Ibid., pp. 296 ff.
46. Westermann, "Arten der Erzählungen," pp. 90, 38.

enigmatic passage. Form criticism has not solved nor can it solve all of the problems presented by this text. However, this little narrative illustrates some of the complicated material which may be opened up to a certain extent by asking form critical questions. It may demonstrate the potential of these questions to uncover some of the background of narrative material which doubtless had a long oral prehistory. Furthermore, our example will show how form criticism, source criticism and traditio-historical research must be carried on in concert with one another.

The form critical analysis of a text should be based on the solution of the source critical questions; that is, if possible, one should know at the outset the answers to the questions of date and authorship. In this case, our text stems from one or more of the pentateuchal sources (for example, the Yahwist or the Elohist).

Various solutions to the source critical questions have been proposed, but no consensus has been reached. On the basis of duplicates and repetitions in the story, Gunkel concluded that the story was composed of elements from the two older sources, J and E,[47] and many scholars have followed his lead. Eissfeldt attributes most of the story to his even more ancient L (for the "Lay" source), and the remainder to J.[48] More recently Karl Elliger,[49] Gerhard von Rad[50] and John L. McKenzie[51] have argued persuasively that the story as a whole stems from the Yahwist, and that the unevenness, duplications, and possible repetitions in the story stem from multiple *oral* traditions. Since it seems to be a safe working hypothesis of cautious source criticism that one should not attribute material to various literary sources unless he can demonstrate the literary affinities of that material with a specific source, we accept this story as stemming essentially if not entirely from the Yahwist.

---

47. Gunkel, *Genesis*, pp. 359 ff.
48. O. Eissfeldt, *Hexateuch-Synopse* (1922; reprint ed., Leipzig: J. C. Hinrichs, 1962), pp. 66 ff.
49. Karl Elliger, "Der Jacobskampf am Jabbok: Gen. 32:33 ff. als hermeneutisches Problem," *ZTK* 48 (1951): 1–31.
50. von Rad, *Genesis*, pp. 314–321.
51. John L. McKenzie, "Jacob at Peniel: Gen. 32:24–32," *CBQ* 25 (1963): 71–76.

In spite of some disagreement it is generally conceded that this story belongs to one of the oldest literary documents of the Pentateuch, if not J then some even more ancient document (for example, Eissfeldt's L). And even though some very highly refined literary analyses have been proposed, virtually all agree that a complicated *preliterary* history lies behind the literary history of the narrative. It is the task of form criticism to recover some of the flavor and meaning of the story as it once existed in that oral tradition.

Structure. Our first task is to set the story into its context in the Jacob narrative as a whole. One notices immediately that the story of the patriarch's nocturnal wrestling match has very little in common with the rest of the stories of Jacob. The stubborn, strong hero who is able to hold his own against a numinous being is quite different from the wily trickster who earlier had fled for his life from his brother and in the immediate context is reported to be deathly afraid to face that same brother once again. He is capable of hiding behind first his mother and then his wives and children. The fact that this story stands out to some extent within the Jacob narrative tends to indicate already that it once circulated independently of other parts of that narrative. As we shall see, there is further evidence to support this conclusion.

Furthermore, the story is exceptional as one of the very few occasions when Jacob is subject to divine revelation. For the most part, a decidedly "secular" atmosphere prevails in the stories of Jacob. The exceptions are the story presently before us (Gen. 32:22–32), the account of Jacob's dream at Bethel (Gen. 28:10–22), and the very brief notice about Jacob's encounter with "God's army" (Gen. 32:1–2). Thus the stories of Jacob at Bethel and Peniel stand out clearly and play particularly significant roles in the narrative.[52] The two stories balance one another in the account of Jacob's life. The encounter at Bethel occurs as he is fleeing the land of Canaan from the wrath of his brother, and the episode at Peniel when he is returning. On the first occasion God gives him the promise of land and progeny; on the second occasion he

---

52. Cf. Westermann, "Arten der Erzählungen," pp. 85; von Rad, *Genesis,* p. 38.

survives an encounter with God and is blessed with the new name Israel. This particular structure of the Jacob narrative, in which these two stories play such a key part, probably is to be attributed to the Yahwist. Systematic ordering with a theological motivation in mind is not the result of the haphazard collecting of stories, but the work of a redactor with conscious intentions. Further elaboration of that structuring and those intentions is the task of redaction criticism as it seeks to understand the thought of this particular redactor, the Yahwist.

As we look more closely at the story in its immediate context we see that it is but loosely connected to the material which surrounds it. The first part of chapter 32 describes the preparations for the meeting between Jacob and Esau; chapter 33 describes the meeting itself. The narrative of Jacob at Peniel thus seems to interrupt somewhat the continuity of the story. Furthermore, the transition into the story of the nocturnal encounter is very rough. In 33:21, it is reported that Jacob "lodged that night in the camp." But in the very next verse we hear that he arose that same night and crossed the ford of the Jabbok. These factors lend further support to the conclusion that this narrative once circulated independently of the other Jacob stories.

The text itself now lies before us. Its structure may be outlined as follows:

Jacob's struggle at the Jabbok (Gen. 32:22–32)

   I. Introduction: The Setting (Jacob is left alone at the ford of the Jabbok) (22–24a)
     A. Report of crossing at night (22–23)
     B. Summary of the setting: Jacob is left alone (24a)

  II. The account of the struggle (24b–29)
     A. The fight itself (24b–25)
       1. "A man" wrestled with Jacob until daybreak (24b)
       2. Jacob's thigh put out of joint (25)
     B. The dialogue between Jacob and his antagonist (26–29b)
       1. The antagonist's request to be released and Jacob's demand for a blessing (26)

2. The antagonist asks Jacob's name, then gives
him a new name: Israel (27–28)
3. Jacob asks the antagonist's name and he asks
why Jacob wants to know (29ab)
C. The resolution of the struggle: the antagonist
blesses Jacob (29c)
III. (Further) etiological conclusions (30–32)
A. Place-name etiology: Peniel (30)
B. Etiology of cultic practice (31–32)

Even a cursory reading shows that while our story is short
it is by no means simple. The outline reveals only some of the
complexities. What actually happened? And between whom?
What is the point of the little tale? None of these questions can
be answered in a sentence; indeed, it is difficult if not impossible to paraphrase the story into a consistent and coherent
whole.

It is clear at least that we are dealing with a narrative in
the strict sense.[53] The account includes a setting, characters,
and a tension which is developed to its resolution. But none of
the features of the narrative is unambiguous here. The struggle
occurs at the ford of the Jabbok, but—as we have seen—it is
by no means clear on which side of the river. More important,
the events transpire at night. It is obvious that one of the
characters is Jacob (Israel!); the narrator takes pains to point
out that he was left completely alone. But the identity of his
adversary is by no means self-evident. It is observed almost
casually at the outset that "a man" wrestled with Jacob. But
something very mysterious lies behind this identification. The
antagonist touches Jacob and puts his thigh out of joint; for
some reason he is very anxious to be gone before daybreak.
He refuses to identify himself to Jacob, but he has the power
to bless him. And finally when the struggle is ended the patriarch declares that he has seen God face to face.[54] The narrative
tension is developed from the attack upon the patriarch,[55] but
it moves toward more than one resolution. The tension actually is dissolved when the antagonist blesses Jacob (v. 29), but

53. Cf. Westermann, "Arten der Erzählungen," p. 85.
54. So Gunkel could correctly call the story "Jacob's wrestling with the
deity" (Genesis, pp. 359 ff.).
55. Westermann, "Arten der Erzählungen," p. 85.

there are other conclusions to the story. One climax is reached when Jacob's name is changed to Israel (v. 28), and two other conclusions are given after the narrative itself has come to a close: the explanation of the place-name Peniel, and the account of the origin of a cultic dietary practice.

The "fight" itself is described in a verse and a half (24b–25). It has resulted in a stalemate. The real struggle takes place in the dialogue or argument between Jacob and his adversary (26–29). Taking all the elements of the story together—the setting, the summary of the action, the report of the dialogue, and the conclusions—we are left with a very brief but self-contained narrative.

The unevenness, the complexity, and the multiple meanings preserved in our little story indicate the presence of several layers of tradition. The concise style, the fact that some aspects of the narrative defy interpretation, and the allusions to pre-Israelite ideas show that some stages of the story are indeed very ancient.

Genre. The analysis of the structure has already shown that our text is a *narrative* which has passed through a long history of tradition. The outline reveals the presence of all the essential elements: setting, characterization, and plot. It now remains for us to specify the genre more precisely under the general rubric *narrative,* and to relate that identification to the history of tradition.

Gunkel identified our story as a saga of a particular kind.[56] Several factors support that identification. The events are private rather than public occurrences, there is no possibility that the story was reported by an eyewitness—rather, the perspective is that of a tradition which knows all that it is important to know about the patriarch—and the story no doubt circulated orally before it was written down. The narrative's brevity and conciseness, its independence, and the fact that it reports an encounter between a man and a deity are further indications that it is a saga. As a matter of fact, this particular episode parallels more closely the hero sagas of other cultures than do most of the other stories in Genesis, since it reports the heroic struggle of a man against a superhuman power.

---

56. Gunkel, *Genesis,* pp. 364 ff.

But *saga* is still a very broad classification, and we must be more specific. Since the time of Gunkel, this story and others like it commonly have been designated as etiological sagas. It is clear that we have here not one but *several* etiologies. Taking the last first, there is the explanation of a cultic practice (vv. 31–32), a cultic etiology. We should not be too disturbed that this rationale makes little sense to us. (Why should people refrain from eating the sciatic nerve of an animal because the *patriarch's* thigh was touched at that point?) Popular etiologies seldom are scientific. Next there is the interpretation of the place-name Peniel (v. 30), an etymological etiology. The name means "the face of God," so, people reasoned, it stemmed from the appearance of God face-to-face to someone in antiquity. Third, there is the etymology of the name "Israel" (vv. 27–28). Others have suggested that there is yet another etiology within or beneath the narrative, either the explanation of the lameness of the patriarch[57] or the etiology of a limping cultic dance.[58] However, if the story at one stage in its history was told to account for the lameness of the patriarch or a cultic dance, that meaning has been lost. The other three etiologies are given according to traditional formulas which draw the relationship between the cause (the event in antiquity) and the result (a name or a practice). No such direct relationship is drawn between the lameness of the patriarch and the events, and a cultic dance is not even mentioned as such.

In addition to its several etiological elements, this saga also contains elements commonly—and correctly—associated with myths or fairy tales. Among these are the following: the motif of an attack by a nocturnal "deity" or demon who is afraid of the daylight, the implied magical causation (the adversary puts Jacob's thigh out of joint with a touch), and the notion that one gains power over a deity or demon by knowing his name. (Why else would the opponent refuse to divulge his name to Jacob? One thinks of the fairy tale of Rumpelstiltskin, in which the princess gains control over the little elf by learning his name.)[59]

57. Cf. McKenzie, "Jacob at Peniel: Gen. 32:24–32," p. 72.
58. Cf. von Rad, *Genesis*, p. 318.
59. Gunkel has assembled some of the parallels to these motifs from the folklore of the world (*Genesis*, p. 364).

So, finally, the story cannot be identified in terms of one simple genre, but several. On the surface it appears to be essentially etiological saga, but there are at least three distinct etiologies, as well as motifs from other genres which have been preserved as vestiges of an earlier form (or forms) of the story. The presence of so many diverse genre elements supports the conclusion that the story has indeed passed through a long history of transmission, bringing with it traces of several different environments.

Our task now is to make some suggestions concerning the relationship of the various genre elements to a proposed history of the tradition. We shall confine ourselves here to a few comments about the present form of the story, then the Yahwistic level, and finally the pre-Israelite stratum. It no doubt oversimplifies the history of tradition to speak of three "stages"—the growth of the story over a period of centuries certainly was more complex than such a scheme suggests.[60] But some definite traces of the form of the story at these points in its transmission are discernible and should lead to some understanding of its history.

(a) As it finally stands, the story is a brief but important chapter in the composite "history" of salvation which resulted from the combination of several literary sources. The position of our episode in the Jacob narrative and thus in the completed story is no doubt inherited from the Yahwist, who earlier had himself written such a history on the basis of old oral—and perhaps even written—traditions. The genre of the story at this final stage is etiological saga, a combination of cultic and etymological etiologies, explaining several matters of importance to the writers and their community. It is possible that one or more of the etiological conclusions are later accretions—their relationship to the narrative itself is quite tenuous[61]—but nevertheless they leave the story to us as etiological narrative.

---

60. F. van Trigt discusses the history of the story along slightly different lines. He proposes the following scheme:
   I. The pre-Israelite level.
   II. The Israelite level.
      A. The oral stratum.
      B. The written stratum.
(F. van Trigt, "La signification de la lutte de Jacob prés du Yabboq, Gen. xxxii 23–33," *Oudtestamentische Studiën*, 12 [Leiden: Brill, 1958], pp. 282 ff.)
61. Cf. Westermann, "Arten der Erzählungen," p. 85.

(b) In the Yahwist's work (J), the story also appears as an etiological saga. In the context of that document, the basic themes are the etiology of the name Israel (v. 28) and the report that Jacob won a blessing (v. 29c). These motifs taken together comprise an etiology for the existence of the people of Israel. The etiology of Israel not only is more integrally related to the narrative itself than are the two other etiologies (vv. 30–32); it clearly is more important in the thought of the Yahwist.

The story must have undergone some changes when it became a part of Israelite tradition, and even more changes at the hand of the Yahwist. The explanation of the name Israel probably was not original: it is a distinctively Israelite tradition. Furthermore, it is likely that originally the hero was not even Jacob. And however the original story identified the assailant, by the time of the Yahwist it is assumed that he is the Lord himself.[62]

(c) Though the story was changed when it was taken over into Israelite tradition and polished by the Yahwist, vestiges of an earlier form remain. These vestiges consist of ideas and motifs which have no place in the theology of the Yahwist in particular or of Israel in general. Israelite religion—at least in theory if not always in actual practice—left no room for nocturnal demons who are afraid of the daylight, or divine beings who can be held at bay by a mere human being. Ideas of magical causation are foreign to her thought.[63] According to Israel, one cannot control a being—human or divine—simply by knowing his name. Thus it is unlikely that these facets of the story would have originated with Israel. Before the story was appropriated into Israelite tradition it probably once related how a nocturnal demon or deity attacked a man in the night and the man struggled to gain power over the god or to gain some of his power by learning his name or winning a blessing.[64] Some sense of the mysterious importance of names is retained by the Yahwist and those who followed him. (Indeed, awe of the divine name increased in Israel to the point that it was not to be spoken at all.) However, the story

---

62. Cf. von Rad, *Genesis*, pp. 317 ff.
63. Cf. ibid., pp. 315 ff.
64. Cf. ibid., p. 316; Gunkel, *Genesis*, p. 362.

as we now have it focuses not primarily upon the name of the adversary but upon the name "Israel."

It is no longer possible to define the genre of the old pre-Israelite story with certainty. Most form critics have reconstructed the original story as an etiology. But just which parts of the story are "original"? We are no longer as confident about our answers to that question as Gunkel was, but the following observations seem reasonable: The story did not originally exist as part of a broader narrative context, but as an independent saga with—at the very least—strong overtones of the myth and fairy tale; the etiology of Israel was not part of the story; very likely the tale was an etiology associated with the supposed place of the struggle.

Setting. Just as our story preserves elements of several distinct genres, so it also retains traces of various settings, a different one for each stage in its transmission. Our discussion of the setting should thus parallel the scheme suggested under the examination of the genre, without in any sense implying that we have thereby captured the full history of the passage.

The settings of both the final form of the unit and of the Yahwist's version of the story—(a) and (b) above—are literary situations. That is, at these stages one must think of writers who are working with a view toward making the old traditions as well as their own ideas available to the community as a whole. Then one must think of Israelites over the generations reading those documents or hearing them read, certainly in the context of cultic ceremonies and probably also in other, less formal, situations.

Some five centuries separate the two literary settings which we have identified. Israel's position in the world of the ancient Near East as well as many of her own institutions changed remarkably over that span of time. The Yahwist probably worked not long before 900 B.C., at a time when Israelites were still basking in the accomplishments of David and Solomon and confident about Israel's destiny as a nation. The literary complex of which our story is a small part received its final form in the postexilic religious community which lived with the memories of the Babylonian exile, on a much-reduced land of Judah. In view of these differences, it is actually surprising how little the story was changed over those centuries. Two things help to explain this fact. First, ancient Israel—like most other communities of faith—was very reluctant to change religious literature once it had been committed to writing. Second, while the historical situation had changed dramatically, the *settings* of both the Yahwist and the final redactor of the Pentateuch are actually quite similar. Both are writers dealing with old traditions for the sake of the community. There are, to be sure, significant differences between these two which should not be overlooked. However, the further elaboration of the historical circumstances, the setting, and the theological perspectives of these writers is the task of literary criticism and redaction criticism as they look at the documents—including their form critical aspects—as a whole.[65]

We turn now to the question of the setting of the story in the pre-Israelite oral tradition. Concerning such stories Gunkel said, "The legends [sagas] of worship in Genesis we may assume with the greatest certainty to have originated in the places of which they treat. The same may be said of other legends [sagas] which ascribe names to definite places."[66] There are indications that our story originated at a cultic center near the ford of the Jabbok, and was circulated by the cultic personnel and the worshipers there. Considerable interest is shown in the location of the events and the name of the place, though the precise spot has been obscured somewhat as the story grew and became disassociated from the holy place. The tale may have been related as a regular part of the ritual at the sanctuary, but its use would not have been confined to official services. Sagas belong to the people who hear them and retell them. It is even possible, as Gunkel supposed, that such stories were passed on by a professional class of popular "story tellers."[67]

Intention. Etiological sagas by definition intend to explain the origin of some facet of present existence by reference to an event in the past; that is their purpose. But we certainly

65. See especially Gerhard von Rad, "The Form Critical Problem of the Hexateuch," in *The Problem of the Hexateuch and Other Essays.*
66. Gunkel, *The Legends of Genesis,* p. 91.
67. Ibid., p. 41.

would not suggest that the point of Genesis 32:22–32 is exhausted by saying its intention is to account for the origin of two names and a cultic practice. Let us look more deeply into the question first by making some general comments about the intention of sagas and then returning to our outline of the story's history, this time reversing our order to take the oldest level first.

We shall certainly be led astray if we expect sagas to give us history; that is not their intention. The men who told and heard and then recorded sagas had not yet learned how to ask the historian's questions. No value judgment is involved in this observation. Saga as a mode of communication is not necessarily inferior to history, nor is it superior; it is just different, based on a different set of assumptions and operating within its own framework. Actually the saga is less concerned with the past than the present. The etiological saga begins as an attempt to deal with some facet of *present* reality. On the other hand, sagas are not the product of poetic fantasy.[68] They grapple with the questions of present life not in terms of generalizations or theories or abstractions but in terms of what they understand to be specific past events—"historical" events in the sense that they are assumed to have happened only once in time and space—which give shape to the present. Sagas, at least those which we find in the Old Testament, mean to deal with ultimate questions. They are not to be seen as *critical* reflections upon ultimate questions, but rather as expressions of Israel's self-understanding. They are, in short, one of the languages of faith. Thus von Rad can say: "All sagas as we have them are concerned much less with men than with God. God is everywhere the real narrative subject, so to speak, of the saga—or rather, its inner subject; men are never important for their own sakes, but always as objects of the divine activity; as those who both affirm and deny God and his command."[69]

As the story was circulated in the old pre-Israelite tradition, it reflected upon ultimate questions—matters of life and death—in a way which is no longer meaningful for us, nor, for

68. von Rad, *Genesis*, p. 31.
69. Ibid., pp. 34–35.

that matter, for ancient Israel herself. As the story originally belonged to the holy place, it reflected upon the awesomeness of that location. It probably meant to explain not only the origin of its name but—more important—how it first was discovered that the site was holy, for in antiquity one did not simply *designate* a place as holy but *discovered* its sacredness. Further, the old saga was an attempt to come to grips with the mysterious and threatening powers which men perceived about them. It articulates an understanding of a world inhabited by such powers and susceptible to control through magical causation.

At the level of Israelite tradition, seen here in the work of the Yahwist, the story deals with equally mysterious matters, such as the question of the relationship between Israel and her God. It no longer receives its meaning by virtue of its relationship to the local cult, but within its broader narrative context.[70] The story, we have said, is still an etiology. But it would be misleading to think of etiology here as a kind of primitive science, a way of supplying answers to the questions of the curious about origins. The story does more than explain the origin of the name "Israel." Above all, it means to give expression to a certain pre-understanding of Israel's existence: Israel is the one who has striven with God and man! Israel—man and nation—has seen God face-to-face and not only lived but been blessed. That is the greatest mystery. How it could be so is not answered in full. Certainly the generations of faithful Israelites who heard this story were able to affirm that what had happened to Jacob was true, because it also had happened to them.

Most of the interests of the Yahwist seem to have been retained in the final form of the story. What is added is an even deeper concern to preserve *all* the tradition. So what must have been a relatively clear outline in the Yahwistic document has become very complicated because of the combination of several documents and tradition. But the final redactors of this material were willing to sacrifice many things—including clarity —for the sake of completeness. They have thus passed on to us traditions which they themselves no longer fully understood

---

70. Ibid., p. 19.

(for example, the etiology of the dietary practice, which is mentioned nowhere else in the Old Testament). Though their efforts at completeness make our task difficult, we may be grateful for their work. *"For no stage in this work's long period of growth is really obsolete; something of each phase has been conserved and passed on as enduring until the Hexateuch attained its final form."*[71]

PROPHETIC LITERATURE

What did it mean to be a prophet in ancient Israel? How did the prophet and those about him understand his role? What was the relationship of the prophet to the life and institutions of his time? How can we understand the always powerful but often enigmatic words of the prophets? More often than not we are puzzled as we attempt to find our way through the maze of sayings and speeches and reports which simply are run together in the prophetic books. But we can begin to gain insight into these and other questions through an understanding of the language of the prophets. In fact, our *only* avenue to the prophets and their thought lies through their words—and the reports about them—which are preserved primarily in the prophetic books.

We have become accustomed to regarding the prophets as the great individual and innovative thinkers of Israel. To a great extent this is true. They were creative, and each one was different. But there is another side which must be the basis for our beginning. The prophets, as all other creative individuals, were part of a tradition, and they used the language and the forms of expression of their own time and place. How else could they be understood? More specifically, they ordered their words in ways which were appropriate to the role which they served. Furthermore, they held in common certain of the theological traditions of ancient Israel. (It is the task of a history of traditions to recover those traditions and locate each prophet within them.)

Our task here is to provide a basis for understanding their language, in particular, the genres in which they clothed their messages. So we should look for that which is *typical*—not

---

71. Ibid., p. 27; cf. also Gunkel, *The Legends of Genesis*, pp. 130–31.

what is always present or ought to be there—in the speeches of these men. Nothing binds them together in a continuum as their genres of speech do. Or, from our perspective in the twentieth century, the only way we can determine the ideas and presuppositions which make them a group is through examining the consistent elements in the ways they expressed themselves. In this endeavor we are not trying to recover the ideal and hypothetical "prophet" by means of a "standard" prophetic genre or genres; we are looking for that continuity which should aid us in understanding each individual.

Gunkel's Contributions

The first attempt to understand the genres of prophetic literature was made by Gunkel, but the results of his work in this area were not as decisive or definitive as his investigations of the narratives and the cultic poetry. He did not produce a work on the prophets comparable to his commentaries on Genesis and the Psalms. His studies of the prophets were for the most part of an introductory character.[72] But in these general works he laid the foundation for what was to follow. His main contribution was in showing us the right questions to ask.

Gunkel emphasized that one should first attempt to determine the original speech unit[73] and give up the idea of the prophetic books as systematic compositions by authors. The importance of distinguishing the originally independent units from one another and then analyzing each has also been stressed by Sigmund Mowinckel. Especially in the prophetic books, one must learn to ignore the chapter and verse divisions which often do not correspond to the changes in the subject matter.[74]

72. "Die Propheten als Schriftsteller und Dichter," in *Die Schriften des Alten Testaments,* ed. H. Gunkel, et al., 2nd ed. (Göttingen: Vandenhoeck & Ruprecht, 1923), Vol. 2, pt. 2, pp. xxxiv–lxx; "Propheten II, seit Amos," RGG[1], cols. 1866–86; *Die Propheten* (Göttingen: Vandenhoeck & Ruprecht, 1917), especially chapter 4, "Schriftstellerei und Formensprache der Propheten," pp. 104–40.
73. Gunkel, "Die Propheten als Schriftsteller und Dichter," pp. xxxiv ff.
74. S. Mowinckel, *Prophecy and Tradition: The Prophetic Books in the Light of the Study of the Growth and History of the Tradition* (Oslo: I Kommisjon Hos Jacob Dybwad, 1946), pp. 37 ff. Mowinckel cites a number of examples to support this point.

Gunkel also emphasized that the prophets originally were speakers and not writers.[75] Though he was not the first to recognize this fact,[76] he was the first to use this insight as the basis for a methodology. He recognized a great many different genres in the prophetic literature, both "prophetic" genres and types borrowed from other spheres of life.

The genres used by the prophets did not remain static over the centuries. Gunkel could discern the general lines of their development in the history of the prophetic movement. The early prophets uttered brief oracles, while later prophets learned to compose longer speeches. What had begun as poetry became prose as prophets developed from ecstatics to preachers and religious thinkers.[77]

Gunkel summarized the main prophetic genres as follows: "Numerous types are found conjoined in the prophetic writings —the vision in narrative form, the prophetic oracles, the discourse [better, "speech" for the German *Rede*] (in many forms). Among these last mentioned, the oldest is that which foretells the future, and may either be the threat or the promise; the invective, upbraiding sin; the exhortation, calling to well-doing, and many others."[78] Though he considered the oracle and the vision report very significant since they stemmed from the prophetic revelatory experiences, recent discussions have focused upon his categories *threat, promise* and *invective*. Gunkel considered these to be classifications according to the content of the prophetic speeches. He regarded the threat and the promise as the oldest and most distinctive prophetic genres. Through them the prophet describes or announces the future in terms of salvation (the promise), or disaster (the threat).[79] He thought of the invective as a genre distinct from the others, a relatively late development, and borrowed from the legal procedure.[80]

Most of Gunkel's observations were basically sound in spite of the fact that they must be corrected and improved in the

75. Gunkel, "Die Propheten als Schriftsteller und Dichter," pp. xxxvi ff.
76. For a highly useful history of the study of the prophetic genres, cf. Claus Westermann, *Basic Forms of Prophetic Speech*, pp. 13–89.
77. Gunkel, "Die Propheten als Schriftsteller und Dichter," pp. xxxix–xlii.
78. Gunkel, "Fundamental Problems of Hebrew Literary History," p. 60.
79. Gunkel, "Die Propheten als Schriftsteller und Dichter," p. xlvi.
80. Ibid., p. lxii.

light of recent investigations. In particular, many have questioned the adequacy of the terms *threat* and *promise* to describe the genres which Gunkel had in mind. Most of his interpretation of the invective has been rejected. Different terminology has come into use which we must correlate with Gunkel's language if we are to understand the form critical studies of the prophets. Most important, we should retain from Gunkel's studies his attention to the individual units within the literature, his emphasis upon the oral origin of the prophetic word, and his observation that in the prophetic speeches we find not one genre, but a great many genres from all spheres of Israelite life.

A General View

With very few exceptions, the genres within the prophetic books fall into three main categories, according to both form (structure) and content. Westermann[81] has recognized these categories by consistently applying Gunkel's basic form critical questions: Who speaks? To whom does he speak? What takes place in this speaking, or what is aimed at?[82] (This last question corresponds to our inquiry concerning the intention of the genre.) When one applies these questions to the prophetic books, he discovers there *accounts, prayers,* and *speeches.* The usefulness and the limitations of each of these terms to organize the prophetic genres should now be examined.

Account is a good neutral term to describe the occasional first or third person reports of the activities of the prophets. Some of these accounts take the form of narratives. Jeremiah 26, for example, is a real third person narrative, reporting the temple speech of Jeremiah, the reaction by the people, and the unsuccessful effort of the priests and prophets to condemn Jeremiah to death. Isaiah 36–39 contains some historical narratives. Usually the narratives are combined with the reported speeches of the prophets. Jeremiah 32 is a first person narrative (autobiographical style) in which the prophet himself

---

81. Westermann, *Basic Forms of Prophetic Speech,* pp. 90–98. In the summary which follows we are indebted to Westermann's analysis.
82. Cf. ibid., p. 93; Gunkel, "Fundamental Problems of Hebrew Literary History," p. 62.

reports how he purchased a field as a sign of Israel's future. The narrative includes the speeches which interpreted the actions. Many accounts simply supply the framework around a speech, reporting the circumstances in which it was received or delivered. The superscription—the heading of a book which dates the prophet—serves essentially that same function for an entire book.

Some of these accounts appear to belong distinctively to the prophetic role. Examples of these are the vision report, the report of the prophetic sign act, and some of the formulas which introduce prophetic speeches.

Relatively few *prayers*—words directed by man to God—are found in the prophetic books. The best-known examples are the complaints of Jeremiah in which he bewailed his lot and asked for help from the Lord. (See, for example, Jer. 12, 15:15 ff., and 17:14 ff.) But there are others which follow—as do the complaints of Jeremiah—the patterns of various types of psalms. There are three hymnic fragments in the Book of Amos (4:13, 5:8–9, and 9:5–6).

Most of the units within the prophetic books fall under the general category *speeches,* in which the prophet himself addresses Israel, a group within Israel, an individual, or a foreign nation. The term "speech" is misleading, however, if one thinks in terms of a long formal composition. As one can readily see in the early prophets particularly, their speeches usually are brief and poetic utterances. There is a spontaneity about their work which makes it clear that they did not act as orators.[83] The main characteristics of the speeches will be examined more fully below.

When one begins to recognize even the broad categories he is on the way to finding the individual units within a prophetic book. Changes in person (for example, from second person address to a first or third person account) and intention often are sure signs that a new unit has begun. These criteria must be used in conjunction with others, such as changes in content and the introductory and concluding formulas, but they provide a beginning.[84] Furthermore, these broad categories often provide data for the study of the literary critical

83. Cf. Mowinckel, *Prophecy and Tradition,* p. 40.
84. Cf. ibid., pp. 55 ff.

and redaction critical question. Third person reports *about* the prophet—such as superscriptions—by their very style, structure, and intention make no claim to be the words of the prophet.

Messenger Speech

The prophets stand before Israel and speak what they say is the very word of God. What they utter they claim was first uttered to them by the Lord, so quite often they are able to quote God directly. This major characteristic of the language of the prophets, evident on virtually every page of the books which preserve their words, has led to the conclusion that the prophetic speeches are *messenger speeches*.[85]

Many factors support the conclusion that the prophetic language is the speech of a messenger. In the accounts of their vocations, the prophets make it very clear that they are called to speak God's word: "Then the Lord put forth his hand and touched my mouth; and the Lord said to me 'Behold, I have put my words in your mouth'" (Jer. 1:9).[86] The same point is conveyed by a great many of the formulas which the prophets employ in their speeches, especially in the very common messenger formula, "Thus says the Lord." Nothing identifies the prophetic word as messenger speech so clearly as this stereotyped phrase which recurs constantly throughout all the prophetic literature. Furthermore, the accounts of the activities of the prophets, both in the prophetic books and elsewhere, report their claim to be spokesmen for Yahweh: "But Micaiah said, 'As the Lord lives what the Lord says to me, that I will speak'" (1 Kings 22:14). To be sure, there is not always agreement concerning the actual word from God in a particular situation (see Jeremiah 28), but there can be no doubt about the prophet's claim to be speaking that word. The identification of prophetic speech with messenger speech is also supported by the parallels of their language to that of nonprophetic messengers, both as reported in the Old Testament narratives and as seen in the ancient Near East generally.

85. See especially James F. Ross, "The Prophet as Yahweh's Messenger," in *Israel's Prophetic Heritage*, ed. Bernhard W. Anderson and Walter Harrelson (New York: Harper, 1962), pp. 98–107; Westermann, *Basic Forms of Prophetic Speech*, pp. 98–128.
86. See also Isa. 6:8–9, Ezek. 2:8–3:11.

The verbs for sending a messenger are the same in both cases.[87] Some have argued further that the form (structure) of prophetic speech parallels that of the message delivered by the messenger.[88] However, this final point requires further investigation, especially in terms of the ancient Near Eastern parallels.

So prophetic speech in general may be described as *messenger speech.* This means above all that what the prophet says is in the strict sense a message—not from the prophet himself to the hearers, but from God by means of the messenger to the people. (This observation holds whether or not the structure of prophetic language always follows the structure of profane letters.) It implies, furthermore, that the distinctively prophetic role is that of messenger of Yahweh.

But while the term *messenger speech* is satisfactory as a general characterization of the words and hence of the role of the prophet, it has its limitations. The prophets expressed themselves by means of a great many genres of speech, many of which are related only more or less directly to the messenger speech. Thus one must investigate the genre of each individual unit in order to ascertain its background and intention. While the role which is both distinctively and consistently the prophetic one is that of the messenger, it would be a mistake to insist too strongly on a single role. The prophets served many functions, and conceived their tasks in different ways. At points they intercede with God for man (see Amos 7:1–3, Isaiah 6:11), at times they seem to preach, and perhaps some even served in specifically cultic offices.

The recognition of the messenger style of the prophetic language helps to clarify the confusion arising from the use of the terms *oracle* and *speech* for the prophetic words. An oracle is a direct word of God, originally the short utterance in response to an inquiry. Ordinarily, the prophet reports the oracle—the revealed word—but in his reporting it or speaking it to the people it has become a message from God. "From the form-critical point of view it may be said—though it means

87. Ross, "The Prophet as Yahweh's Messenger," pp. 99 ff.
88. Westermann, *Basic Forms of Prophetic Speech,* esp. p. 111. On the other hand, cf. Klaus Koch, *The Growth of the Biblical Tradition,* pp. 216 ff.

to simplify matters—that the prophetic saying is that 'oracle' clothed in the form of the 'messenger-message' from God."[89]

The Prophetic Word as Announcement

What transpires when the prophetic messenger speaks? What is he trying to accomplish in his speaking? What is the thrust or the point of his message? Obviously there is no simple answer to this question, since the prophetic movement spanned several centuries, and each prophet faced a different situation with a different message. Furthermore, the prophets couched those messages in a great many different genres of speech. These facts only make it all the more surprising how often the same general answer can be given to the question of the intention of the prophetic speeches. What transpires most commonly in those speeches is *announcement* or *proclamation* concerning the immediate future.

These announcements, whether they are addressed to individuals, to Israel, or to foreign nations, are easily divided into two categories: the announcement of disaster or the announcement of well-being. Taken in their context and in the light of the prophetic understanding of God and of history, it is more accurate to describe these as *announcements of judgment* and *announcements of salvation*.[90] When the prophets announce impending trouble, they do not simply announce disaster, but disaster because of the sins of the individual or the nation addressed. Hence, the disaster is a judgment. When they announce well-being, they are speaking of what God is about to do on behalf of his people. Hence their good news is an announcement of salvation. When they speak as they often do about the future, it is not just any future, but a future which God brings about. Thus one should use theological terms to describe their speeches.

The prophetic announcements of judgment and salvation are not to be confused with predictions, though there are some similarities in style. It should be emphasized that the prophet always appears to be speaking about the immediate future in the light of his own situation and in the light of the history of the people of God. The basic distinction between predic-

---

89. Mowinckel, *Prophecy and Tradition*, p. 40.
90. Cf. Westermann, *Basic Forms of Prophetic Speech*, pp. 94 ff.

tions and prophetic announcements lies in the conception of the power of the prophetic word. As the prophets see it, their words are not speculations about coming events, but the very word of God about the future. That word—the word of God spoken through the mouth of the prophet—has the power to create history. "The prophets did not predict the course of history. By their threatening word they believed they were making the future disaster inevitable."[91] Jeremiah, for example, is commissioned not to utter words which may or may not be compelling to his hearers, but through his speaking "to pluck up and to break down, to destroy and to overthrow, to build and to plant" (Jer. 2:10; cf. also the discussion of Amos 1:1–2 below, p.74). Because it was felt that the prophetic word was a powerful force, those who disagreed with the prophets did not simply ignore them, but tried to hush them up.

What we are calling here—following Westermann and others —announcement of judgment and salvation Gunkel labeled the *threat* and the *promise*.[92] What we have already said shows that the term *threat* is not strong enough for the prophet's bad news concerning the future. It is too weak primarily because it implies a conditional element, for example, that disaster— judgment—will come if the people do not repent.[93] At least in the announcements of judgment themselves, no such condition is stated or implied. The future had already been decided. The purpose of the announcement of judgment was to set that future into motion and to make it clear beyond a shadow of a doubt that the coming trouble was Yahweh's judgment upon his people for very good reasons. If and when such announcements also served as warnings to the people to cease giving Yahweh reasons for judgment, a secondary interpretation had been given to them.

In addition to what we are now calling the announcement of judgment and the announcement of salvation Gunkel recog-

---

91. G. Fohrer, "Remarks on Modern Interpretation of the Prophets," *JBL* 80 (1961): 318.

92. Koch prefers instead of the term *announcement* simply to call them *prophecies* (*The Growth of the Biblical Tradition*, p. 210).

93. Cf. Westermann, *Basic Forms of Prophetic Speech*, pp. 65 ff., for a discussion of this as well as other arguments in favor of the term *announcement of judgment*.

nized an independent genre which he called the *invective* or
the *reproach*. He meant to characterize with these terms the
passages in which the prophets described the crimes and sins of
the people with stinging words and harsh detail. It has been
recognized, however, that such units do not represent an independent genre, nor are they—as he implied—a late development
in the history of prophetic literature. One finds such re-
proaches as a part of the speeches of the preclassical prophets
reported in the historical books. Indeed, such descriptions of
the crimes of the people are found as one part—a genre element
—of the prophetic announcements of judgment, early and late.
What Gunkel called the invective or the reproach actually
serves to specify the *reasons* for the judgment which is announced, as the following example shows:

> ⁹Hear this, you heads of the house of Jacob
>> and rulers of the house of Israel,
>> who abhor justice
>> and pervert all equity,
> ¹⁰who build Zion with blood
>> and Jerusalem with wrong.
> ¹¹Its heads give judgment for a bribe,
>> its priests teach for hire,
>> its prophets divine for money;
>> yet they lean upon the Lord and say,
>> "Is not the Lord in the midst of us?
>> No evil shall come upon us."
> ¹²Therefore because of you
>> Zion shall be plowed as a field;
>> Jerusalem shall become a heap of ruins,
>> and the mountain of the house [of the Lord]
>> a wooded height (Micah 3:9-12).

The speech begins with an introductory call to hear or
summons to attention—a common formula—which also names
the addressees (v. 9a). Then as the addressees are described
their sins are listed (vv. 9b–11). This is invective and reproach, but in the context it is more than that. In verse 12 the
prophet turns his attention to the future, announcing judgment
upon the city of Jerusalem. The relationship between the
sins and the judgment is drawn clearly and unambiguously by
the "therefore" which begins verse 12.

This text is by no means an isolated example. Its structure recurs dozens of times in the prophetic speeches. Thus, when the prophet catalogues the crimes of his people he is not just reproaching them or censuring them or denouncing them with invective: he is laying the foundation—giving the reasons—for the announcement of judgment. Within the prophetic view of history, God's judgment is not capricious or irrational, but reasonable. The disaster which is coming is God's response to Israel's failure to obey what had been communicated to her from the beginning.

Within limits, many variations are possible in the announcements of judgment as the prophets struggle to find ways to communicate their basic message. The order of the elements within the genre may vary. In some cases, one finds only the announcement without the reasons, and occasionally even the reasons without a corresponding announcement. In many instances, these facts may be explained by the state of affairs which we find in the prophetic books themselves. Between the time of the original prophetic utterance and the final written form of the books, the speeches have passed through many hands and doubtless many of them are available to us only fragmentarily. Nevertheless, when we look at the prophetic announcements of judgment as a whole, we can agree with Westermann: "The only thing remaining the same throughout all these variations is that which constitutes the essence of the judgment speech directed to Israel—the judgment of God is announced to the people because of specific failures."[94]

---

94. Ibid., p. 176. Westermann proposes a far more detailed structure of the prophetic announcement of judgment to Israel than the outline suggested here. According to that scheme, the speeches begin with an introduction, the reasons consist of an accusation and the development of the accusation, the transition to the announcement of judgment is accomplished with a messenger formula (and usually also "therefore"), and the announcement of judgment itself includes two parts, the intervention of God and the results of the intervention (see esp. pp. 168–76). It is quite true that one can detect precisely this structure in many prophetic speeches, but there are difficulties with such a detailed structure. To begin with, far too many prophetic speeches (including announcements of judgment) fail to conform to the full pattern. More serious is the fact that such a structure, in spite of Westermann's warning to the contrary, conveys the impression that it describes the ideal or the original pattern appropriate for prophetic speech. It is more accurate, it seems to us, to describe the various parts of this structure as elements which very often are used in the genre.

The similarity of the prophetic announcement of judgment to the presuppositions and the patterns of the courtroom process is obvious.[95] Consequently, some have suggested that the origins of the genre lie in Israelite legal procedures. The forms of expression no doubt have been influenced from that direction, and the prophets in some instances actually employ the technical language of the court, but the genre is more specifically rooted in the prophetic situation itself and the particular prophetic assumptions about God and history.

We have focused primarily upon the prophetic announcement of judgment to the people of Israel. Such announcements can also be addressed to specific groups within the nation (see Micah 3:9–11 above), or to single individuals (Amos 7:16–17).[96] There also are announcements of judgment addressed to or concerning foreign nations (Amos 1:3–2:3). On the other hand, announcements of salvation become more and more common in the later prophets. The reasons for God's actions in such announcements are not given so frequently as in the judgment speeches.[97] In all such speeches, the prophet as Yahweh's messenger announces what his Lord is about to do.

Other Genres

Though we have characterized prophetic speech in general as messenger speech and argued that the most distinctly prophetic genres are the announcements, we have emphasized— following Gunkel—that both the prophets and those who recorded their words employed a great many different types of speech and literature. Some of these are closely related to the messenger's announcements. Among these are *vision reports*, in which the prophet described what Yahweh has shown him, but almost without exception they either consist of or include a message, usually an announcement (see Amos 8:1–3). The *report of the prophetic vocation* is a special form of the vision

---

95. Cf. ibid., pp. 135 ff.
96. Westermann argues that the announcement of judgment to the individual is the earlier form.
97. Nevertheless, Koch argues for a basic similarity in the structure of the two kinds of announcements (*The Growth of the Biblical Tradition*, pp. 210–15).

report. In all of the main examples (Isa. 6:1–13, Jer. 1:4–10, Ezek. 2:1–3:16) it is quite clear that the inaugural visions were not reported in order to provide the spiritual biography of the prophet, but for a very special reason. Regardless of the particular experience which lay behind the report, or the personality of the individual prophet, the *reports* of the vocations follow the same basic patterns, employ many of the same linguisitc features, and were presented to accomplish the same purpose: to authenticate the prophet as the messenger entitled to announce God's word.

One also finds *accounts of sign acts,* either by the prophet himself or by those who recorded the traditions about him. As in the vision report the prophet interprets what he has seen, so in the report of the sign act the prophet interprets his actions, thereby once again proclaiming his message (see Isa. 8:1–4, Jer. 19:15, and Ezek. 4–5).

The prophets also utter *admonitions or warnings* of various kinds as well as *woe oracles.* In the admonition, the prophet tells the people what is expected of them if the judgment of God is to be averted: "Seek the Lord and live, lest he break out like fire in the house of Joseph, and it devour, with none to quench it for Bethel . . ." (Amos 5:6). The admonition sometimes has the appearance of a conditional announcement of judgment, but it also takes other forms. *Woe oracle* is the term applied to the prophetic speeches—especially frequent in Isaiah—which begin with the cry "woe," followed by a description of the addressees and usually also an announcement of judgment.[98]

The list of the genres, genre elements and formulas used by the prophets to express themselves is almost endless. Especially important is the use of the technical, legal language of the court process.[99] Some prophetic speeches actually present

98. Westermann, *Basic Forms of Prophetic Speech,* pp. 190 ff. Westermann interprets the woe oracles as variants of the basic prophetic announcement of judgment, but the question concerning the origin of these speeches must be left open. It is likely that at least some elements of the genre have been borrowed from other spheres of Israelite life. Cf. E. Gerstenberger, "The Woe Oracles of the Prophets," *JBL* 81 (1962): 249, 263.
99. On this point see especially E. von Waldow, *Der traditionsgeschichtliche Hintergrund der prophetischen Gerichtsreden,* BZAW 85 (Berlin: Töpelmann, 1963).

Yahweh as the plaintiff arguing a case against his people:

> ¹Hear what the Lord says:
> Arise, plead your case before the mountains,
>   and let the hills hear your voice.
> ²Hear, you mountains, the controversy [lawsuit]
>   of the Lord,
>   and you enduring foundations of the earth;
> for the Lord has a controversy [lawsuit]
>   with his people,
>   and he will contend with Israel (Micah 6:1-2).

In this text we hear the official summons to appear in court; the speech of the accuser follows (6:3-5). The language of the courtroom is used quite frequently in Second Isaiah (see especially Isa. 43:8 ff.). The prophets also allude frequently to the laws which Israel is supposed to obey. Since the prophets were so concerned about the crimes of their people, their use of legal language is completely understandable.

One finds genres both borrowed from and copied from those of the cult. Hymns of praise and psalms of complaint have been mentioned already. In addition, numerous other formulas and genres from Israel's life of worship are represented. In Amos 4:4, for instance, we find a call to worship which has been transformed into an indictment of worship:

> "Come to Bethel, and transgress;
>   to Gilgal, and multiply transgression;
> bring your sacrifices every morning,
>   your tithes every three days; . . ."

The prophets also used or wrote proverbs and sayings such as the ones found in wisdom literature, as well as types and expressions from everyday life. One finds a series of sayings characterizing the relationship between cause and effect in Amos 3:3 ff., a parable in Isaiah 5:1-7, and a proverbial saying is quoted and reinterpreted in Ezekiel 18:2-4. Amos even found it useful to compose a song which he specifically identified as a dirge (or lament):

> ¹Hear this word which I take up
>   over you in lamentation,

67

FORM CRITICISM OF THE OLD TESTAMENT

O house of Israel:
²"Fallen, no more to rise,
    is the virgin Israel;
forsaken on her land,
    with none to raise her up" (Amos 5:1–2).

One sings such songs over the dead, at the funeral. The judgment of the Lord upon Israel is so certain that Amos can already begin the funeral. Thus the dirge becomes a very graphic means of announcing judgment.

Setting

We have discussed a few of the genres of speech and literature in the prophetic books and considered the structure and intention of some of the main types. It remains for us to comment briefly on the setting of these genres in the life of ancient Israel. Since a great many prophets over a period of several centuries employed many different genres, most of them taken over from other areas of life, and the prophetic speeches later were collected and finally written down in books, the question of setting is by no means a simple one. With regard to this issue in the prophetic literature we have to consider in most cases the following points: (1) the setting in the life (experience and activity) of the prophet himself, (2) the background of the prophetic language, and (3) the place of the speech in later oral and written tradition.

(1) The question of the setting of prophetic speech in the life of the prophet himself has its historical, sociological, and even psychological aspects. At least the historical situation is relatively clear. What we characterize as the prophetic movement arose in Israel not long before the establishment of the monarchy and died soon after the state was destroyed by the Babylonians. The precise limits are more difficult to establish. Second Isaiah clearly is a prophet, but even earlier in the work of Ezekiel we can recognize that the prophetic modes of speech—and with them the prophetic role itself—are changing into what eventually would become apocalyptic literature. Nevertheless, most of the individual prophets can be placed into their historical contexts and related to their predecessors and successors.

The question of the sociological setting of the prophet

speeches is more difficult. One may say, quite simply, that their setting is *prophecy*. That is true enough: there was "an institution" which we could call prophecy. But how shall we characterize that institution, and what was its relationship to other institutions in Israel? This institution, as all others, changed over the centuries. At least in some periods there were bands of prophets organized around a leader, as the stories of Elijah and Elisha show us. We also hear of other groups of prophets as well as outstanding individuals such as Nathan who seemed to be attached more or less officially to the royal court. But the issue is least clear when it becomes most important, with the classical prophets. Consequently, different proposals have been offered concerning the role of the prophet. While an earlier generation of biblical scholars tended to assume that prophets were always and everywhere opposed to the priests and argued that most of the cultic language in the prophetic books was added later, more recently some scholars, studying Israel's worship and recognizing the cultic language which the prophets themselves must have used, have argued that prophets must have served official functions in the cult. It is true that there is evidence for a relationship between cultic ceremonies and some prophets, but the prophets were not basically or primarily cultic personnel performing official duties, as were the priests. Very few of the prophetic speeches which have been handed down to us were uttered in the context of worship. Other scholars noticing the use of wisdom language and expressions have argued for a close relationship between the prophets and teachers. But one has only to compare the Book of Isaiah, for example, with the Book of Proverbs to recognize that a basically different situation lies behind the two.

The continuity of the prophetic language and traditions shows us that prophecy was indeed an institution. To be sure, it was not always officially recognized or sanctioned. Some prophets had disciples (Isa. 8:16 ff.), and all of them sooner or later had followers who took their words seriously. How else can we explain the preservation of their words? The situation which lies behind prophetic speech is the actual oral delivery of that speech by the prophet; but where, and to whom, and on what occasion? We find prophets speaking inside the temple, but also everywhere else they find an audience; to kings, but also to any and everyone in Israel; on special occasions, but also whenever a word must be spoken. Apparently the prophets sensed few if any restrictions upon their activities. Since their authority came not from men but from God, they spoke whenever and wherever they felt compelled to do so.

The prophets allude repeatedly to another situation in their activity, the private occasion when they received from Yahweh the word which they later delivered publicly. But they tell us very little about those experiences. We have no way even of knowing whether or not a specific revelatory experience lies behind every prophetic use of the phrase, "Thus says the Lord," or "The Lord showed me. . . ." The prophets were much more interested in proclaiming their messages than in telling about their experiences. The living situation is that time and place when the prophet opened his mouth to speak.

(2) As we have seen, most if not all of the genres used by the prophets were taken over or adapted from other situations. This applies not only to the obviously borrowed genres, such as proverbial wisdom sayings or the language of the cult, but to the specifically "prophetic genres" as well, such as the announcements of judgment and salvation, and to the messenger style in which most of the speeches are cast. The prophetic messenger formula, "Thus says the Lord," and perhaps other aspects of the prophetic language as well, had their roots in the ancient Near Eastern mode of communication through messengers. Announcements of judgment were influenced by Israelite legal procedure. Just as one cannot fully understand the prophets apart from their historical situations, so one gains insight into the meaning of their words when the background of their language is recognized for what it often is: the technical language of a particular institution in ancient Israel. Thus one should inquire not only into the setting of the prophetic speeches themselves, but into the original settings of their language as well.

(3) The prophetic words continued to live long after they were spoken. When the speeches which had been delivered over the years on various and sundry occasions were collected and then written down, they were given a new and different

life. In many cases the collected speeches first circulated among the disciples of the prophet. Later, the speeches lived as literature and thus became the property of the community as a whole. As the speeches were handed on first orally and then in writing, many additions were made. Traditions *about* the life and work of the prophet were added by those who knew him. Later speeches and other compositions were attributed to the prophet and included. All this material was organized, sometimes haphazardly and sometimes coherently, and finally provided with a framework—perhaps no more than an introductory notice, the superscription to the book. A speech which originally served one purpose may serve a different one in the context of the book.

Often one can distinguish the words of the original prophet from the work of later tradition. When this is possible, one can recognize not only *that* the prophetic words continued to live, but *how* they lived in the community of faith. When the Israelites in Babylonian captivity read the Book of Amos, for example, the old announcements of judgment took on new meaning. Their validity was not challenged or denied, but affirmed. The affirmation that the Lord had indeed judged Israel became the basis for a new beginning.

Some Examples

Amos 1:1–2:
[1]The words of Amos, who was among the shepherds of Tekoa, which he saw concerning Israel in the days of Uzziah king of Judah and in the days of Jeroboam the son of Joash, king of Israel, two years before the earthquake. [2]And he said:

> "The Lord roars from Zion,
>   and utters his voice from Jerusalem;
> the pastures of the shepherds mourn,
>   and the top of Carmel withers."

Structure.

    I. Superscription $(1–2a\alpha)$
          A. Title of the book ("The words of Amos . . .") $(1a\alpha)$
          B. Elaboration of the title $(1a\beta b)$
               1. Concerning Amos $(1a\beta)$
               2. Concerning the words $(1a\gamma)$

These two verses should be considered together as one unit, though the unit has two distinct parts. In the final redaction of the book, these two elements have been combined by the transitional "and he said" to serve together as the introduction to the book as a whole.[100] All of the prophetic books begin with superscriptions, but this is one of the most elaborate. It includes the title of the book, the name of the prophet, his occupation, his home, the subject of his words, and two versions of the date. The complexity and the unusual syntax indicate that this verse is the result of literary growth and expansion.[101] An earlier superscription probably included only the following words: "The words of Amos of Tekoa, which he saw concerning Israel two years before the earthquake."[102]

The other phrases in the superscription probably were added at different times. The royal date which coordinates the reign of a king of Israel with that of a king of Judah follows the pattern commonly used in the Deuteronomistic History (Joshua through 2 Kings), and may have been inserted here by a Deuteronomistic editor of the Book of Amos.[103] The reference to the prophet's occupation and the date in the time of Jeroboam of Israel probably depend upon the very reliable narrative account of one of the prophet's experiences in Amos 7:10–15. The structure of the motto is symmetrical, reflecting somewhat the patterns of both the Old Testament reports of

---

100. Cf. A. Weiser, *Die Profetie des Amos, BZAW* 53 (Berlin: Töpelmann, 1929): 252 ff.

101. Ibid., p. 252; H. W. Wolff, *Dodekapropheton: Amos*, Biblischer Kommentar 14 (Neukirchen: Neukirchener, 1967), p. 146.

102. Cf. James L. Mays, *Amos: A Commentary* (Philadelphia: Westminster, 1967), pp. 18 ff.

103. Cf. ibid., p. 18.

Yahweh's theophany and the prophetic announcements of judgment against the nation.

Genre. Two basically different genres, superscription and motto, have been combined to serve together as the introduction to the Book of Amos. The superscription is a *literary* genre in the proper sense; that is, it developed at the stage of the written collection of the prophetic words. One does not need such a formal heading unless he has a book. However, most literary genres have preliterary backgrounds, and the superscription is no exception. It is parallel to and probably also rooted in the titles of collections of wisdom sayings (Cf. Proverbs 30:1, Job 31:40).[104]

To characterize verse 2 as a motto is to say that it is a statement prefixed to a literary work to characterize both its contents and tone. That the motto is an *introduction* to announcements of judgment and not such an announcement itself is seen by its general character, the fact that no reasons for judgment are given, and the hymnic style. This particular motto bears the marks of two types of speech: (1) The report of the theophany which described the coming of Yahweh and the terrible results of his coming,[105] and (2) the prophetic announcement of judgment. The similarity to the former is more obvious.

Setting. In their final form, these two verses stem from the redactional activity of the circles which preserved and finally edited the words of Amos. As they stand, the combined superscription and motto presuppose the existence of at least the body of the book itself with the possible exception of the epilogue (9:8c ff.) and a few other late additions.

Both the superscription and the motto, however, reflect earlier settings. An earlier—and shorter—version of the superscription probably existed, and may have circulated at the head of the collection of vision reports in Amos 7–9. This suggestion is based on the fact that the title refers to the words which Amos "saw"[106] as one sees in a vision. The motto is

---

104. Wolff, *Dodekapropheton: Amos,* p. 149.
105. Cf. ibid., pp. 147 ff.; J. Jeremias, *Theophanie,* WMANT 10, (Neukirchen: Neukirchener, 1965), pp. 113 ff.
106. Cf. Weiser, *Die Profetie des Amos,* p. 255; Wolff, *Dodekapropheton: Amos,* pp. 146 ff.

either an adaptation or a copy of the formal cultic language which was used by cultic circles in Jerusalem to describe the awesome appearance of Yahweh on Mount Zion. The references to Zion and Jerusalem, as well as the fact that the structure of this pronouncement parallels so closely the traditions about Yahweh's theophany support this conclusion.[107]

Intention. The introduction as a whole functions to identify and date the prophet, to characterize his words, and to set the tone for the book. The purpose of the superscription is not primarily biographical, though the writer certainly has some of the historian's concerns. He wants to get the facts straight and record them. But the intention is deeper. It is very important to establish the concrete historical setting for the historically oriented prophetic words. Those words were addressed to a particular time, which is established with the first words of the book. In addition to setting the tone of the book, the motto recalls the traditions concerning Yahweh's self-revelation and emphasizes the terror and power of Yahweh's coming through his word spoken by the prophet. The old tradition spoke of the Lord's appearance and the resulting upheaval in nature. According to this pronouncement, the Lord appears through his voice. That voice is present and powerful, so it was thought, in the words of the prophet Amos. Thus, as a part of the introduction to the book, the motto not only describes the words which are to follow but authenticates them.

Amos 3:1–2:

[1]Hear this word that the Lord has spoken against you, O people of Israel, against the whole family which I brought up out of the land of Egypt: [2]"You only have I known of all the families of the earth; therefore I will punish you for all your iniquities [Literally: I will visit upon you all your sins]."

Structure.

I.	Expanded call to attention	(1)
	A. Call to attention	(1aα)
	B. Elaboration of the call	(1aβ–c)

---

107. Cf. Weiser, *Die Profetie des Amos*, pp. 84 ff.

       1. Concerning the word ("which Yahweh
          has spoken. . . .")   (1aβ)
       2. Concerning the addressee   (1b, c)
          a. Identification of the addressee
             ("against you, O people of Israel")
          b. Description of the addressee with a
             formula from the history of salvation

II. Speech of Yahweh (Messenger style)   (2)
    A. "Reasons" for judgment: Yaweh's election
       of Israel   (2a)
    B. Announcement of judgment   (2b)
      1. Transition ("therefore")
      2. Announcement ("I will visit upon you all
         your sins.")

The introductory call to attention indicates quite clearly that a new unit has begun. This little speech is a self-contained entity which is to be distinguished from what precedes and follows[108] on the basis of both form and content. However, in the context of the collected speeches of Amos, the general and somewhat reflective theological character of this unit allows it to serve as a fitting introduction to the collection of announcements of judgment in Amos 3:1–6:14.

In general, this speech follows the pattern of the announcements of judgment. The broad structure of introductory call, reasons for judgment, and announcement of judgment introduced by "therefore" is visible, but the reasons are only implied in a paradoxical way.[109] That is to say, instead of the more typical indictment of Israel by means of very specific descriptions of concrete transgressions, Israel is reminded of her special relationship with Yahweh; the election is recalled in stereotyped language from the covenant tradition. It is not self-evident that election (Israel's being known by Yahweh) is a reason for judgment, but the structure which links Israel's election to the announcement of judgment with "therefore" implies that the reasons lie precisely in that election itself. Judgment is coming because Israel has not fulfilled her cove-

---

108. Cf. Weiser, *Die Profetie des Amos*, pp. 116 ff.; Wolff, *Dodekapropheton: Amos*, pp. 212–13.
109. Cf. Weiser, *Die Profetie des Amos*, pp. 122 ff.

nant responsibilities; a special relationship involves special responsibilities.

In other ways the structure of this little speech is somewhat distinctive. The introduction is more elaborate than most; there is no messenger formula as such, and no oracle formula ("says the Lord"), but there is an indication of the source of the word (1a). The announcement of judgment with its allusion to reasons ("your sins") is general and abstract.[110] The hearers are not told how or when Yahweh will intervene, only that he will. There is no reference to the effects of his intervention.

A number of stereotyped formulas occur. Among these are the call to attention (which also occurs in Amos 4:1 and 5:1), the covenant-election terminology (1c, 2a), and possibly also this particular formulation of the announcement of judgment (2b).

Genre. In spite of some distinctive features, the structure and intention of this unit mark it as a messenger speach. As we have seen, there is no messenger formula ("Thus says the Lord") as such, nor does this particular introductory call to attention identify the unit as a messenger speech, since such calls may begin speeches of different kinds. Nevertheless, the elaboration of the call to attention identifies the words which follow as the words of the Lord, and then the prophet—standing in the role of a messenger—quotes Yahweh directly. More specifically, the unit is a prophetic announcement of judgment against the people of Israel. The prophet's introduction to the word of Yahweh is given in verse 1; in verse 2 Yahweh speaks that word in the first person through the prophet.

Setting. As a speech genre, this address belongs quite specifically to the prophetic role in ancient Israel. Here Amos is doing what only a prophet does: proclaiming judgment in the name of Yahweh. This particular speech would have been delivered to the people in a context which assumed two things: (1) knowledge and acceptance of the salvation traditions concerning the exodus and the covenant, and (2) the sinful self-satisfaction of the people. At least in its final form,

---

110. Ibid.

the announcement applies to all Israel, North and South, but this fact may be the result of editorial additions. The phrase which applies the judgment unambiguously to all Israel (1b) may have been added later. (The expression introduces a somewhat disruptive shift in person within a single sentence —from a third person reference to Yahweh to first person— and it is well known that Amos addressed himself to the Northern kingdom.) As literature the unit serves as the introduction to the collection of speeches in Amos 3:1–6:14. That is, it owes its particular location within the Book of Amos to those who collected and organized the speeches of the prophet.

Intention. Generally, the function of this speech is to announce and to motivate judgment upon Israel for her sins. More specifically, the speech implies that Israel's election makes her particularly culpable for her crimes. The prophet has taken the assumptions of his listeners (Yahweh has elected us) and drawn a radically different conclusion (judgment is coming).[111] Thus in addition to announcing judgment, the speech serves to destroy the false notion that election exempts Israel from punishment. Since the sins are not specifically described, the emphasis is upon God's punishment based on the covenant relationship.[112]

---

111. Cf. ibid.
112. Cf. ibid., p. 121.

Epilogue

We indicated at the beginning of chapter II that it was impossible to examine here all the genres of the Old Testament. We have considered only two general categories, narratives and prophetic literature, and examined only a few of the main genres of each. At this point our range of vision may be broadened somewhat by noting briefly some of the other genres widely used in the Old Testament and some of the important form critical studies of those genres. These comments should serve only to emphasize the depth and the breadth of the literature and traditions of ancient Israel. We shall limit ourselves to a few observations about the legal material, the religious poetry, and wisdom literature.

Laws and legal procedures are necessary parts of any society. Certainly those who have learned to identify the Old Testament—or part of it—as "the Law" will know that ancient Israel was no exception to this rule. While one finds references to laws from one end of the Old Testament to the other, most of the formal legal regulations are concentrated in a few codes in the Pentateuch: the decalogue (Exod. 20; cf. also Deut. 5:6-21), the ritual decalogue (Exod. 34:14-26), the book of the covenant (Exod. 21-23), the holiness code (Lev. 17-26), and the laws in the Book of Deuteronomy.

It was Albrecht Alt who laid the foundation for understanding the relationship of the Old Testament laws to the life and institutions of ancient Israel.[1] According to Old Testament tradition, he observed, all the laws and ordinances originated in the period immediately before Israel entered the land of Canaan, and were handed down by God to Moses. But the laws themselves are far from consistent, as they would

---

1. Albrecht Alt, "The Origins of Israelite Law," in *Essays on Old Testament History and Religion*, pp. 101-71.

have been had they been established at the same time. Literary criticism had solved some of the questions concerning the history of the laws by dating the individual codes in relationship to their narrative context. However, literary criticism alone can only recover the oldest *literary* stages in the history of the law, it cannot recover the origins: "The making of law is basically not a literary process at all, but part of the life of a community."[2] Alt thus applied the techniques developed by Gunkel to the law codes and the individual laws.

He recognized that there were two basically different types of law. The first is casuistic—or case law. Each law has two parts, a condition and a legal conclusion, a protasis and an apodasis, and it is expressed in the third person: "If a man steals an ox or a sheep and kills it or sells it, he shall pay five oxen for an ox and four sheep for a sheep" (Exod. 22:1). One finds a great many such laws in the book of the covenant, arranged more or less according to content. Both in terms of their structure and their content, they parallel very closely the non-Israelite law codes of the ancient Near East. The content of these laws assumes a settled agricultural society with established legal traditions and practices. Alt therefore concluded that the origin of these laws was to be found outside of Israel, that Israel appropriated both the genre and many of the individual laws from the Canaanites who were in Palestine before them.

The other type he called apodictic law. Their formulation is quite different from that of the case laws. They do not have two parts, but one, a short categorical statement in the second person: "Whoever strikes a man so that he dies shall be put to death" (Exod. 21:12). The content of these laws is as unconditional as their formulation. They all deal with crimes punishable by death or a curse. Since Alt found no ancient Near Eastern parallels to the apodictic laws, he concluded that they were uniquely Israelite, and that their categorical nature was based directly upon the will of Yahweh.

Considerable attention has been given to the Old Testament laws since the time of Alt, and many of his conclusions— especially those concerning the apodictic laws—have been questioned. Since there is nothing unique about the apodictic

---

2. Ibid., p. 110.

style as such—it is a common way of regulating behavior and giving instructions—it has been argued that they are not uniquely Israelite nor originally cultic in nature, but stem from the family and tribal life of the seminomadic groups of the ancient Near East.[3] Nevertheless, Alt has shown us the questions which must be posed if one is to recover the preliterary history of the Old Testament laws.

Some of the most important contributions of form criticism have come in the study of Israelite cultic poetry and song, most of which is found in the Book of Psalms. Before the work of Gunkel, scholars had been concerned primarily with the date and authorship of each psalm. The general scholarly consensus placed the great majority of these songs in the postexilic community, and considered the Book of Psalms the hymnbook of the second temple. Only the last part of this consensus remains, and only in a very modified form: The Book of Psalms *as a collection* finally took shape during the postexilic period and was used as a part of the worship of that community. Gunkel's studies of the psalms[4] not only opened the way to a new understanding of the conceptions which inform the psalms and to an understanding of the place of the individual psalms in the life of the people, but also to the recognition that many of these songs are older than the postexilic collection.

Gunkel recognized that one has only to read through the Book of Psalms to be impressed with the similarities of many of these songs to one another. The same expressions, motifs, and even structures recur over and over again. On the basis of these similar structures and expressions, he was able to establish the main genres of the psalms and to draw conclusions concerning the setting of each type in the life of Israel. The main genres were: hymns sung in praise of Yahweh in the sanctuary on high occasions, the communal lament sung by the assembled congregation at times of need, the individual lament used at times of personal need or trouble, the individual song of thanksgiving sung when a person brought a thank

---

3. See especially E. Gerstenberger, *Wesen und Herkunft des "Apodiktischen Rechts,"* WMANT 20 (Neukirchen: Neukirchener, 1965). Some of Gerstenberger's conclusions are summarized in "Covenant and Commandment," *JBL* 84 (1965): 38–51.

4. Hermann Gunkel, *Die Psalmen übersetzt und erklärt;* Hermann Gunkel and Joachim Begrich, *Einleitung in die Psalmen.*

offering, the royal psalms, and some other minor genres, including among others the communal thanksgiving and the victory song. Gunkel concluded that most—if not all—of these types, including the individual laments and thanksgiving songs, arose and were originally used in cultic ceremonies. He argued, however, that a great many of the extant psalms actually were the compositions of pious individuals imitating the cultic types.

A great deal of debate has taken place around this last point. Mowinckel, whose works are clearly the most significant since those of Gunkel,[5] extended Gunkel's research in the direction of a "cult functional" evaluation in which each and every psalm was placed in a formal religious ceremony. He also reconstructed an "enthronement festival of Yahweh" with which he associated many of the psalms. It is Mowinckel, in particular, who has located a great many of the psalms in the actual cultus of the temple of Solomon. In this respect, we feel, he has actually followed the form critical evidence more consistently than Gunkel himself did.

Gunkel's categories have been modified by some, but not always improved;[6] still they remain as the basis for all studies of the psalms. One category in particular requires clarification. What Gunkel called *laments* actually are *complaints*. We would reserve the term lament for the dirge, or the funeral song; when the complaints are sung there is still hope that death or disaster may be averted, and God is petitioned to save the individual or the community.

In recent years, the area of Old Testament wisdom sayings and literature (Proverbs, Job, and Ecclesiastes in particular) has been studied intensively. *Wisdom* means a great many different things. It is the knowledge based on experience contained in the advice given a son by his father, a pupil by his teacher, an apprentice by the master craftsman. It is also the insight conveyed in a lengthy didactic poem. Wisdom is universal. People always and everywhere have attempted to pass on the common sense learned from experience by means of short, pithy, memorable sayings. The Old Testament pre-

---

5. See especially S. Mowinckel, *Psalmenstudien;* and *The Psalms in Israel's Worship.*

6 Claus Westermann, *The Praise of God in the Psalms,* trans. Keith R. Crim (Richmond: John Knox, 1965).

serves a wealth of such sayings (especially in the Book of Proverbs) as well as a number of formal compositions which serve essentially the same function.

What is the setting of this Old Testament wisdom material? One cannot begin to answer this question without first distinguishing between the different genres. There are first of all short sayings of many kinds. Consensus has not been reached concerning the terminology for such sayings, but it is recognized that there are many types. *Sayings* is the most comprehensive term. Some of these are proverbs: "A living dog is better than a dead lion" (Eccles. 9:4). Many make their point—as does this one—by means of comparisons: one thing is better than another. One also finds numerical sayings, riddles, and what appear to be artificial wisdom sayings, that is, literary compositions after the style of the popular sayings. Then there are the lengthy compositions such as Job and Ecclesiastes. The setting of the short proverbial sayings is the broadest one possible. They arose and were used in everyday life. As people met and talked, as the elders sat at the gate and discussed the state of affairs, and as people communicated the practical knowledge necessary for life in general or for a particular task, the ancient Israelite often expressed himself— as we do—in clichés or concise sayings. Such wisdom seldom if ever can be traced to a particular author.

Eventually scribes and teachers began to assemble collections of these sayings and to write sayings of their own. Many of the numerical sayings seem to be the result of self-conscious reflection:

> [18]Three things are too wonderful for me;
>   four I do not understand:
> [19]the way of an eagle in the sky,
>   the way of a serpent on a rock,
>   the way of a ship on the high seas,
>   and the way of a man with a maiden
> (Prov. 30:18–19).

Such collections and compositions must have been used in the formal instruction in the school, probably in connection with the royal court. At the end of a long line of development stand the formal literary wisdom compositions such as Job and Ecclesiastes. Here one can think of writers at their desks, trying to understand the world and their lives, and to communicate their insights creatively.

Some common assumptions hold these diverse literary and oral genres together. Prudence and morality are the watchwords of wisdom. If one wishes to survive and prosper, he must be careful, learn the rules and obey them, and work hard. Wisdom is basically "humanistic"—it is interested in man with all his potential and problems. Its insight into man and history is based not upon a special word from the Lord but upon that knowledge universally available through experience and observation. These assumptions shape the genres of oral and written wisdom, and explain why some of the characteristics of those genres are so universal.

Still, both the genres and the content of Old Testament wisdom developed some specifically Israelite characteristics. Wisdom reflects upon faith as well as morals. The Book of Job attempts to deal with the answer to suffering which had been given by Israelite faith. By the time the Book of Proverbs was taking shape the "common sense" of wisdom thought was brought into the context of theological reflection. There can be no contradiction, it was argued, between the knowledge gained from experience and that given by revelation: "The fear of the Lord is the beginning of knowledge . . ." (Prov. 1:7).

Form criticism does not provide the key to all the puzzles of the Old Testament, but it is one of the essential tools for those who would understand this ancient and foreign book. To be sure, problems remain for form criticism as a discipline. There are many disagreements concerning terminology, especially in the definition of genres. Many of these are only quarrels over the choice of words, but some reflect substantive differences. Many areas remain relatively untouched by form critical analysis, for example, the apocalyptic literature. Nevertheless, as we have tried to demonstrate, it is not only necessary but possible for all students of the Old Testament to ask the form critical questions and expect to gain insight into the relationship of the texts before them to the life and institutions of ancient Israel.

Bibliography

FORM CRITICAL METHODOLOGY

GUNKEL, HERMANN. "Die israelitische Literatur." Reprint. Darmstadt: Wissenschaftliche Buchgesellschaft, 1963.

————. "Fundamental Problems of Hebrew Literary History" in *What Remains of the Old Testament*. Trans. A. K. Dallas. New York: Macmillan, 1928. Pp. 57–68.

KOCH, KLAUS. *The Growth of the Biblical Tradition: The Form-Critical Method*. Trans. S. M. Cupitt. New York: Scribner's, 1969.

NARRATIVE GENRES

GUNKEL, HERMANN. *Genesis, übersetzt und erklärt*. Göttingen: Vandenhoeck & Ruprecht, 3rd edition, 1917, reprinted, 1964. The introduction to this work is translated by W. H. Carruth in *The Legends of Genesis*. New York: Schocken, 1964.

VON RAD, GERHARD. "The Form Critical Problem of the Hexateuch" in *The Problem of the Hexateuch and Other Essays*. Trans. E. W. Trueman Dicken. Edinburgh: Oliver & Boyd Ltd., 1966. Pp. 1–78.

WESTERMANN, CLAUS. "Arten der Erzählungen in der Genesis" in *Forschung am Alten Testament*. Munich: Kaiser, 1964. Pp. 9–91.

PROPHETIC LITERATURE

WESTERMANN, CLAUS. *Basic Forms of Prophetic Speech*. Trans. Hugh Clayton White. Philadelphia: Westminster, 1967.

LEGAL GENRES

ALT, ALBRECHT. "The Origins of Israelite Law" in *Essays on Old Testament History and Religion*. Trans. R. A. Wilson. Garden City: Doubleday, 1967. Pp. 101–71.

THE PSALMS

GUNKEL, HERMANN. *Die Psalmen übersetzt und erklärt*. Göttinger Handkommentar zum Alten Testament, II/2. 4th ed. Göttingen: Vandenhoeck & Ruprecht, 1926.

————, and BEGRICH, JOACHIM. *Einleitung in die Psalmen: Die Gattungen der religosen Lyrik Israels*. 1933; reprint ed. Göttingen: Vandenhoeck & Ruprecht, 1966.

————. *The Psalms: A Form-Critical Introduction*. Trans. Thomas M. Horner. With an introduction by James Muilenburg. Facet Books, Biblical Series 19. Philadelphia: Fortress, 1967.

MOWINCKEL, SIGMUND. *Psalmenstudien*. Oslo, 1921–24. Reprint ed. Amsterdam: P. Schippers, 1961.

————. *The Psalms in Israel's Worship*. Trans. D. R. Ap-Thomas. New York: Abingdon, 1962.

84